THE BOOK OF
DARTINGTON PARISH

MICHAEL MACLENING

HALSGROVE

First published in Great Britain in 2007

British Library Cataloguing-in-Publication Data.
A CIP record for this title is available from the British Library.

ISBN 978 184114 623 2

HALSGROVE

Halsgrove House
Ryelands Farm Industrial Estate
Bagley Green, Wellington, Somerset TA21 9PZ
Tel: 01823 653777
Fax: 01823 216796
email: sales@halsgrove.com
website: www.halsgrove.com

Frontispiece photograph: *Dartington Church tower.
Dating from the fourteenth century,
in early 1944 it was used as a radio
communications centre by American troops.*

Printed and bound in Great Britain by CPI Antony Rowe Ltd, Chippenham

*This book is dedicated to those servicemen who were born or
who lived in the parish, who gave their lives during the First
and Second World Wars and who are buried in distant
lands, beneath ocean waves or have no known grave.
Several of them I knew.*

The First World War	The Second World War
P.H. Barter	*R.F. Arscott*
J.C.Budd, MM	*R.J.C. Holder*
E.R.A.C. Cox, MC	*W. Hunter*
W.C. Edmonds	*W.F. Kerswell*
R.W.D. Hill	*W.G. Sercombe*
J.H. Hodge	*G.C. Stafford, DFM*
H.P. Kellock	*K.C. Walton*
W.H.G. Kerley	*H.C. Williams*
F. Lock	
H.M. Swears	
F.J. Wakeham	
J. Western	

What's 30mph?

Why must you hurry through our narrow lanes,
has your accelerator got all the brains?
You pass me by like a meteor shower,
that wheel has given you all the power.
Do you ever think of slowing down
instead of driving like a clown?
Because on your tombstone it might say,
'He lived to kill for many a day'!

William G. MacLening
Resident

CONTENTS

Acknowledgements

*T*he Book of Dartington* would not have been possible without those who have contributed photographs and material, have kindly loaned family albums, searched through lofts and helped in the project. My sincere thanks to the following:

Mary Bartlett, Dartington
Tony and Wendy Beard (née Selleck), Widecombe-in-the-Moor
Daisy Beaty (née Bickford), America
Ruth Bennett (née Holwell) and Michael Bennett (dec'd), Totnes
Gwen Brooks (née James), Dartington
Betty Clark (née Sercombe), Marldon, Paignton
Pat Crook (née Winson), Fife, Scotland
Jeanette Denham (née Blatchford), Totnes
Stuart Giles, Dartington
Pamela Gorman (née Sandrey), Dartington
Peter and Margaret Hodge (née James), Ivybridge
Edgar and Beryl Hodge (née Gill), Dartington
David and Kate James, Taunton
Jack and Margaret James, Buckfastleigh
Rosemarie Johansen (née Kerswell), Totnes
Valerie Keel (née Lake), Dartington
Ivan Llewellyn, South Brent
William (Bill) and Tessa (dec'd) MacLening, Dartington
John and Cecile Milton MBE (née MacLening), Petersfield, Hampshire
Tony and Molly Newson (née Auty), Totnes
Betty Osborne (née James), Dartington
Ivy Parnell (née Edmonds), Dartington
Rosemary Piller (née Tuffnell), Torquay
Stan and Cynthia Quaintance (née Taylor), Dartington
Julia Roberts (née Morgan), Dartington
Chris and Lisa Williams (née Osborne), Dartington
Mary Wood, Dartington
Wendy Wyatt (née Giles), Dartington

Dartington Hall Trust
Dartington Rural Archives
Devon Library
Devon Records Office
The Commonwealth War Graves Commission
Totnes Image Bank and Rural Archive
Totnes Museum

Introduction

My first inclination to write a book about the village where I was born came in the year 2000, but it drifted away until the following year, when the impulse returned. The idea was to have a history of Dartington parish, for present and future generations and for those who, like me, have moved away from the village. Over the years several books have been written by various people on Dartington Hall and the Elmhirst's, but none that I am aware of about the parish, its inhabitants and events.

I casually mentioned the idea to my family, and also to a couple of Dartington 'maids' I had known since my schooldays. The response was encouraging – 'What a good idea', 'Yes, go for it' – so the enthusiasm was rekindled!

As my research began, interesting facts and stories emerged. Most people were very helpful and, although one or two were not interested, I knew there would be a few disappointments along the way – life is never straightforward. I did not set a time in which to finish the project, but within a couple of years material and photographs began to accumulate – time to seriously think about a publisher! Having read a number of books published by Halsgrove and been impressed with their format, I contacted them and, from day one, they were very helpful, sending me information. The day Katy Charge (the commissioning editor) came to see me I was a little apprehensive, never having written a book before, but she ok'd my material, which boosted my confidence.

Although I left the village 50 years ago, for 30 years I frequently returned to visit my parents, and saw many changes take place, some of them not so good. The green fields where we had played as children became vast housing estates, industries disappeared and the once quiet village roads were filled with traffic and parked vehicles. What the future holds for the village in the twenty-first century only time will tell, although it will no doubt be joined with Totnes, thus, sadly, losing its identity. Progress is a word frequently used today, but for those dwindling few who remember the village of over 60 years ago, the use of that word is debatable!

I have enjoyed working on this project and meeting and reminiscing with 'old faces', and I hope *The Book of Dartington Parish* will be of interest not only to present-day parishioners, but to future generations of village residents, giving an insight into the people and events of bygone years.

Mike MacLening
2007

The Author

Michael 'Mac' MacLening was born in the village and lived here for 22 years. His Swiss-born mother and Kentish father arrived in 1932 and resided in the parish for over 50 years, 45 of them in Cott Cross Cottage.

Educated at the Shinner's Bridge Primary School, under the guidance of Misses Murch, Nichols and Matthews, Mike then moved on to Redworth (Totnes) Secondary School, leaving in December 1949 at the age of 15.

Joining British Railways as an engine cleaner at the Newton Abbot depot (73 locomotives), Mike qualified as a fireman in July 1951, a job which took him on routes to Plymouth, Penzance, Kingswear, Exeter, Taunton, Bristol and Westbury and on the Moretonhampstead, Ashburton and Kingsbridge branch lines, as well as to 'banking' duties at Totnes. Two years' National Service in the Royal Artillery interrupted his railway career.

On marrying his Salcombe-born wife, Betty, they set up home in Kingskerswell, closer to his place of work. As diesel began to replace steam, Newton Abbot depot became one of the first on the western region to be affected, and by mid-1962 almost all steam locos had gone. The last three went in January 1963 and, with fewer diesel-powered locomotives allocated, redundancies began.

Following the death of his young son, Mike left the railway in April '63 and moved to Surrey with his wife and daughter, where he lived for 33 years, working as a telephone engineer. Tragedy struck again in September '64 with the loss of a 4^1/$_2$-month-old son. The couple adopted a six-week-old 'son' the following year.

A keen footballer, Mike played in the South Devon and Farnborough (Hants) District Leagues, but did not pursue the offer of a trial with Brentford FC. Reaching the age of 37, he decided to hang up his boots and was persuaded to become manager of a boys' football team for the next seven years.

His wife was a maternity nurse at Aldershot Hospital for five years, and at Frimley Park Hospital for over 21 years.

When he retired from British Telecom, the family moved back to Devon, living in Ivybridge where, sadly, Betty died of cancer 2^1/$_2$ years later. Mike's daughter, Judith, lives close by and his son, Paul, in Southampton. He has two grandsons and four granddaughters.

Mike's many hobbies include philately, collecting coins and banknotes from all over the world and reading.

He has travelled extensively.

The author.

... during his football days.

CHAPTER 1

A Brief History of Dartington Parish Families and the Poor of the Parish

Dartington is situated two miles from Totnes, the A384 from Buckfastleigh and A385 from Plymouth meeting at Shinner's Bridge, now the centre of the village. Its buildings date from the fourteenth century and are the most important medieval examples in the West of England.

Dartington – the Homestead of the Meadow by the River Dart – is first mentioned in the registers of Shaftesbury Abbey in AD883. In that year, the Saxon lady Beorgwyn handed over her lands at Shaftesbury and accepted, from King Egbert of Wessex, his offer of lands at Dartington-ham. In the Domesday Book (1086) this is listed as one of the manors held by William of Falaise, one of William the Conqueror's Norman captains.

The manor was bounded to the north and east by the River Dart and to the west by the manors of Dean, Rattery, Follaton and the Borough of Totnes. The 12-mile boundary of the parish, with its $4^{1}/_{2}$ square miles of agricultural land and woodland, has changed little since that time. There was no village; the manor consisted of the lord's demesne and the scattered farms and hamlets of Tigley, Venton, Allerton, Westcombe, Hood, Week, Cott and Puddaven.

By 1113, Dartington had come into the hands of the Fitz Martin family, who built the 9ft stone deer park wall, much of which still stands today, and the first stone church, of which only the fourteenth-century tower remains. It was during this time that Johannes Cott, a wealthy Dartmouth merchant beginning to ply his trade, gave his name to the inn (1320) and hamlet, converting the original cottages into a staging post. On 13 October 1333 he was admitted a Freeman of Totnes. The inn provided refreshment to passing customers and lodging for those using the only packhorse route from Ashburton to Totnes.

Dartington lay in the centre of one of the oldest trade routes in the country. On Dartmoor, tin mining and farming were thriving industries, along with the production of hides and wool, and the Dart was renowned for its salmon – two local fishermen had to render 80 salmon from the river yearly to the lord. Although most traffic was by packhorse until after

The centre of Dartington village in the 1990s.

1800, oxen were often used to haul heavy loads up steep hills, and many farmers kept a yoke of oxen for hire, to bring extra cash to their farms. Before a bridge was built, roads from the north led down to the ford at Staverton, up to Dartington Hall, then down to what is now Shinner's Bridge, fording the Bidwell Brook (then known as the Gulle), and up the hill towards Cott, from where there were two ways to the sea. The first of these was through Staple and down to the Queen's Arms, to which building, originally used for the drying and bailing of wool, a tidal estuary carried barges before the weir for Totnes Mill was built in 1585.

Sailors used to lodge at 'New Houses', some of the oldest cottages in the parish, situated on the left half-way up the hill towards the Cott Inn. The other route to the sea ran past this inn, along Longcause, down Barracks Hill, up through the North Gate into Totnes and down through the walled town to the port, where goods were loaded onto ships.

In 1348 the Fitz Martin occupation came to an end and, not long afterwards, the property reverted to the Crown.

In 1384 Richard II granted the Manor of Dartington to his half-brother, John Holand, and much of the present building is due to him, including the vast double quadrangle, of which only one court (the present courtyard) remains, the banqueting (great) hall, the tower, the kitchens, the east and west wings and the barn (now a theatre). Apart from some ruined arches, the second court, on the south side of

Yarner Beacon, which overlooks the village.

the banqueting hall, no longer survives; however, there is definite evidence of a tilting yard, and it is known that John Holand was a jouster. Created Earl of Huntington in 1387 and Duke of Exeter ten years later, he made Dartington his principal seat in Devon. In 1400 he was executed for conspiring against Richard II's successor, and some 60 years later, during the War of the Roses, the family forfeited Dartington to the Crown.

During the troublous times before 1483, the Church of Dartington (Hall) was sacked and pillaged, and the earliest churchwardens' accounts of that date tell of the expenses incurred in restoration. An apparently insignificant entry in these registers is perhaps amusing to decipher. With subscriptions being raised for the restoration, an odd contribution

The medieval Dartington Hall Church which, except for the tower, was dismantled in 1878.

The church nave, 1876.

of 3s.4d. from the then rector was promptly expended on drinks for the workmen at the Cott Inn. This seems innocent enough, except that another entry reveals that, with the price of cider in those days at 6s.8d. a pipe, the rector's 3s.4d. provided 60 gallons of cider for this little outing!

In 1558 Dartington Manor included Ashridge in Harberton, a great part of Rattery parish, lands at Cockington and possibly Gullaford in Staverton. All that part of Dartington between Malt Mill Bridge and Cott and between Puddaven and Copland was included in a sub-manor known as Northford, of which Longcause was the probable manor-house. Alienated from Dartington Manor, this was held by various owners, including the Fortescues, Fowells, Saverys and other well-known families. At that time Hood was known as 'Stockdown', Droridge as 'Drigidge', and Billany as 'Bellinghay', while Thrushley Remeston, Skilvingscole and one or two other farms remain unidentified. The road along the Bidwell Valley from Totnes turned up the hill (Clay Lane) at Puddaven to join the road at Yarde's Grave Cross. The present road past the Queen's Arms had not been constructed, which probably explains why the thatched Puddaven cottage now stands below the raised road. The Plymouth (A385) road from Shinner's Bridge onwards was probably only a lane.

Dartington passed through various hands until, in 1559, it was purchased by Sir Arthur Champernowne of Modbury, the younger son of Sir Philip Champernowne, whose mother, a Carew, was connected to the Royal House of Tudor. When younger, Sir Arthur had been caught up in the family's involvement, begun in 1553, in a plot to prevent Queen Mary's marriage with Philip of Spain. For this, along with a cousin, Gawen Carew, and William Gibbs of Fenton, he had been imprisoned in the Tower for a year, before being pardoned. Sir Arthur's sister, Katherine Champernowne, was mother to Sir Walter Raleigh (b.1552).

Made Vice-Admiral of the West under Elizabeth I, Sir Arthur played a prominent part in preparing for the threat of the Spanish Armada. He was respon-

sible for the seizure of Spanish treasure at Dartmouth and Fowey and for the setting up of Yarner Beacon, one of the series of beacon sites established to alert the country in the event of a Spanish invasion. There were similar sites near Blackawton, Dean Prior, Denbury and Marldon.

Sir Arthur died in 1578 and Gawen, one of his sons, who was Commander of the Light Horse Regiment in Devon, equipped a ship, entirely at his own expense, to join the English fleet against the Armada in 1588.

The building of Totnes weir in 1585, attributed to Gawen, made possible the reclamation of what was left of the marshes which had filled all that part of the valley, turning the Bidwell tidal creek into meadow-land which, even today, is still prone to flooding. The Champernowne family, who had financial interests in Dartmoor tin, retained possession of Dartington for nearly 400 years, during which time a number of alterations were made, including the rebuilding of residential quarters at the end of the banqueting hall, the demolition of the buildings of the south court-yard in the late 1600s and the conversion of the northern half of the main courtyard (the barton) into a farmstead.

When, in 1636, Francis Champernowne, sixth son of Arthur Champernowne, sailed for Maine, New England, from Dartmouth, he left on the map, besides Dartington, several Dartmouth names, which survive to this day.

In 1766 the last male representative of the senior line died, leaving an only daughter. A cousin carried on the succession for another eight years, but died without a son to succeed him, and the estate passed to the Revd Richard Harington, who had married Jane Champernowne, the heiress. Arthur Harington, their son, assumed the name and arms of Champernowne when he succeeded to Dartington. When he died, his son Henry being only four years old, the estate was managed by the Revd Archeacon Froude, Rector of Dartington. He was the father of historian James Anthony Froude and of Richard Hurrell Froude, one of the leaders of the Oxford Movement.

The Dartington Hall buildings fell into disrepair. The banqueting hall roof was taken down for safety in about 1814, the old kitchens were allowed to disin-tegrate and the church was pulled down in 1878, leaving only the tower. Many of the materials, including the pulpit, were used in 1880 to build a new church of similar design beside the road to Buckfastleigh, at Parsonage.

Two marble pillars from the Great Exhibition of 1851 were later placed in St Barnabas Church, which was built in 1855 at the west end of the parish at Brooking (Tigley).

Early in the nineteenth century the highway to Totnes was shifted to its present position, bypassing the Cott Inn and its area of clustered cottages, which

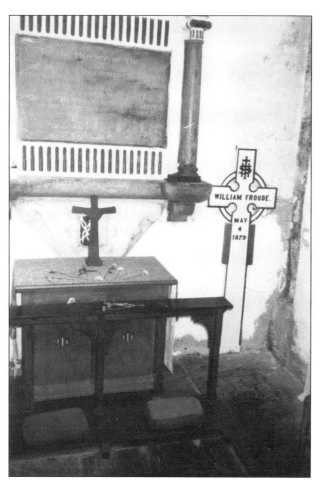

Inside Dartington Hall tower.

Inside the tower, the resting place of Sir Arthur Champernowne, who died in 1578.

by now were thought of as the village. Other dwellings in the parish were still very scattered.

With the decline of the tin and cloth trades and a slump in agriculture, during the late 1870s, following a worldwide recession in trade and a series of bad harvests, Britain fell into a long agricultural depression. Many farmers went bankrupt and had to sell off their land. Drastic reductions in agricultural labour, along with increasing industrial development in towns and cities, took a heavy toll of the population in rural areas. The parish population, 486 in 1801, which had risen to 660 by the middle of the century, now began to decline. Many families died out or moved away; the names Blackler, Mugford, Phillips and Searle were no longer to be found in the parish records of those days, though many others, who had provided continuity since medieval times, still remained; the Millers, Shinners and Windeatts, and later the Barnes, Gill, Hannaford and Hodge families, were still living in the village.

Although 11 generations of Champernownes had lived at the hall since the mid-sixteenth century, they were not a particularly wealthy family (£3,388 income a year in 1872), and at the end of the First World War the harsh realities of their impoverished 5,000-acre estate forced them to dispose of land and outlying properties. Sales in 1919 and 1921 left the

estate extremely run down and buildings derelict. With only 876 acres of fertile farmland remaining, many workers departed to seek their fortunes elsewhere. With the house abandoned, the Champernowne reign was over.

Leonard Knight Elmhirst first viewed Dartington Hall on the afternoon of 4 March 1925. It was in a very dilapidated state, with the banqueting hall and old kitchen in ruins, the private house no longer habitable and the courtyard being used as a farmyard. Only 15 men, women and children remained on the entire estate.

'L.K.', as he became known, was born in 1893, son of a land-owning family in Yorkshire. In 1919, he worked his passage to America as a ship's writer, and studied agriculture at Cornell University in New York state, where, in 1921, he met his future wife, Dorothy Whitney Straight. Born in 1887, Dorothy was the daughter of William C. Whitney, an American statesman, who left her a fortune when she was aged 17. Her husband, Willard, a US Consul with whom she had once travelled to China, died of pneumonia in 1918 while serving with the US Peace Delegation in Paris, leaving her with three children.

Dorothy married Leonard on 4 April 1925 and gave up the comfort of her American home to come to England with him. They purchased the estate for

Restoration work inside the courtyard, 1928.

£30,000 in September 1925 and, happy with his choice, she gave him encouragement and support. Leonard had previously worked with Rabindranath Tagore, the Indian poet, establishing a Rural Reconstruction Department at Tagore's International University in Bengal, India, and was determined to see if a similar venture could be viable in rural England. With only the private house, musty and neglected after four years, still watertight, in June 1926 the Elmhirsts moved in to begin their new adventure!

Extensive restoration and rebuilding were urgent. The banqueting hall had had no roof for over 100 years, the kitchen block was in ruins, the ranges on either side of the courtyard in need of repair and rooms above the entrance tower were in danger of imminent collapse. The abundance of timber, partly an inheritance from the Champernownes, who had had an interest in forestry, meant immediate employment for about 600 men.

Even before the end of 1925, L.K. had outlined a draft for the restoration of the great hall, but six years were to pass before architect William Weir – who directed almost all the reconstructions – started the major task of re-roofing and restoring the hall. He prepared designs along similar lines to those chosen by the original master carpenter in the late-fourteenth century. Although all the timber (except for one tie-beam) had been cut from oak trees growing on the estate several years before, work did not start until 1931 and was completed in 1934. Much of the

work was carried out in the old sawmill, then situated on the present-day car park.

The textile department was founded in 1927 by Herman (Toby) FitzPatrick, who began the setting-up of a small mill equipped with machines which would produce yarn for home-weavers, who would then return the cloth for finishing and marketing. In 1928, carding machinery, a spinning jack and a willey (a machine for cleaning wool and other materials) had been installed in the Ship Studio in the courtyard. There were three assistants. In August 1931, the textile department moved to new premises, built beside Bidwell Brook on the road to Totnes. The sluice-gate regulating the water to turn the large wooden wheel (brought from a Welsh mill) was situated a short distance upstream.

The Elmhirsts, with the help of J.R. (Jock) Curry, developed two farms – Barton, a typical mixed holding, and a new unit built at Old Parsonage, specialising in dairy. Land for woodland and farm use was increased to 4,000 acres. Within ten years, the original farm at Shinner's Bridge was converted to a cider mill (1928), with adjoining orchards, producing fruit for wines and also apple juice – the first commercially produced in England. A large new sawmill, laid out on American lines, was built beside the Plymouth road and further along, at Yarner, a poultry farm, with around 3,000 laying hens and young stock. The textile mill and, across the River Dart at Staverton, a building concern which was to develop world-wide connections, were among the

The textile mill, shortly after its opening in 1931.

commercial enterprises which provided employment and security for hundreds of workers.

The Elmhirsts founded the progressive, co-educational Dartington Hall School, of which W.B. Curry was headmaster from 1931, and an arts centre, established later, was attended by many foreign artists, forced out of their countries during the 1930s because of their political beliefs .

The idea of a school had been central from the beginning, its first prospectus in 1926, entitled 'Outline of an Education Experiment', still remaining a pioneering statement. Originally there were about a dozen pupils, most of them boys aged from seven to 16. Situated in the courtyard, the school was small but significant. Its emphasis on projects, its ideas on self-expression and self-government and its use of the practical activities of the Estate as an essential part of its educational methods, were far in advance of its time. During the next few years the number of pupils slowly increased, but never exceeded 30 before 1931. In 1932 Foxhole School campus was opened.

When the arts department was started in 1934 it was decided to engage a prominent man of the theatre, who would settle on the estate and found a studio. Michael Chekhov was chosen and, with 20 students enrolled for a three-year course, began to direct his Theatre Studio in 1936. Before the days of Arts Council patronage, Dartington laid the foundations of its reputation as an international centre for the arts — the seedbed out of which the present College of Arts was to grow. Chekhov's students included Paul Roger, Yul Brynner and Beatrice Straight; painting classes were given by Mark Tobey, who was later sent by the Elmhirsts to Japan with renowned potter Bernard Leach, who wrote *A Potter's Book*, while at Dartington.

In 1931 the Dartington Hall Trust was established, taking the responsibility for education, the arts and research, while the commercial enterprises were grouped together into a limited company, Dartington Hall Ltd, with directors L.K. Elmhirst, (Chairman), D.W. Elmhirst, F.A.S. Watkin and W.K. Slater DSc.

(Managing Director). There were ten departments: forestry/sawmilling, orchards/cider mill, Barton Farm, Old Parsonage Farm, poultry, textiles, gardens, economics, the laboratory and draughting.

Over 50 new houses were built during the Elmhirst's first ten years, including housing estates at Broom Park (1931) and Huxham's Cross (1932), and Council estates at Beacon View (1929) and Redlake (1935). Although the estate had its own generator and sewage plant, requests for mains sewerage and electricity, needed in particular to power the sawmill, were made to the Parish Council. These services were thus provided in the parish far sooner than they otherwise would have been.

The community around Shinner's Bridge grew fast. In 1925 a Village Hall, built and furnished by subscription as a memorial to those men of the parish who had served in the First World War, was sited next to the four almshouses built in 1835 by Miss Spedding, sister to Mrs Froude, the wife of Archdeacon Froude, rector of the parish. On 15 September 1925, a programme of music was the first entertainment held in the completed hall, which has since been used for jumble sales, whist drives, coffee mornings, bingo, entertainments, public and political meetings, Women's Institute meetings, private receptions and Parish Council meetings.

The grocery store, owned by Canadian-born David Guy and his local wife, moved from Dartington Lodge in 1927 to a new building opposite the village school at Shinner's Bridge. It also became a Post Office, and a petrol station and workshop were added.

In 1935 the Central Offices were opened, and the following year the South Devon pilot artificial insemination scheme, the first in Britain, was set up. The outbreak of war in 1939 brought to an end the initial building boom of the Elmhirsts. The Dartington Hall Estate Committee was founded in 1942 and the following year the first Foundation Day was held. In 1944 Dartington Hall Cattle Breeding Centre was opened and Dartington Joinery Works in 1945.

With the end of the war, housing development started again in the parish, with six wooden 'Swedish Unit' houses built at Newman Crescent during 1945/46. The Adult Education Centre opened in 1947. Major growth took place at the Dartington Hall School and the College of Arts, with the Old Postern education complex built and the textile mill and farms extended.

More housing built by the Trust and by the council and private enterprise included Tolchers in 1950, Droridge in 1960, Hunter's Moon in 1969/70 and Redlake second phase in 1970/71. In 40 years, from 1931 to 1971, the village population more than doubled, from 692 to 1,438, and those figures did not include the 240 college students and 222 at Dartington Hall School who were resident during term time. In 1977 the population had

Digging on the site for the Village Hall, April 1925.

The Village Hall.

reached 1,570 and in 1996, 1,619. The first Dartington Children's Christmas Festival was held in 1951. The cider factory closed in 1952 after only 24 years and the following year Shinner's Bridge House opened as a tea room and the first Dartington Hall Summer School of Music was held.

In 1968, aged 81, Dorothy Elmhirst died and her ashes were scattered in Dartington Hall gardens.

The village school grew as the local population increased. In 1970 Brimhay Nursery School was built as a joint enterprise between the Trust and the County Council, and the Bidwell Brook Special School was built.

Leonard Elmhirst remarried in 1972 to Dr Susanna Isaacs, an ex-school pupil. They moved to Italy for a short time, finally settling in California,

where he died in 1974, aged 80. His ashes were also scattered in Dartington Hall gardens.

Since that time, many of the Trust's original enterprises have closed, including the sawmills, the textile mill, Staverton Builders and Dartington Hall School, which celebrated its 60th anniversary in 1986.

New initiatives established include the Schumacher College, the Dartington Centre, two share farming partnership, Dartington Arts, Dartington Trading Company, Dartington Tech and the Webber's Yard industrial estate on the former sawmill site. Other enterprises are the Rudolf Steiner School at Hood Manor and Park School, in the former junior section of Dartington Hall School at Aller Park.

Families

In 1674 there were approximately 40,000 families living in Devon. In 1801, the year of the first census, the figure had risen to 73,391, an increase of 85 per cent in four generations. Most families were yeoman farmers, including many in Dartington, where the numerous farms within the parish have declined over the last century, their grazing ground having become housing estates.

Many family names have been prominent in Dartington for centuries, several of them linked through marriage. Some families, though not necessarily related, had the same surname, Barnes, Hodge and Parnell being three examples.

Until the last century it was common for three or

The grocery store, with petrol pump, 1927.

The petrol station in the late 1920s, with David Guy (left) and Fred Giles.

four generations of a family to live in the village for 100 years or more. Bidlake, one of the oldest family names recorded in the parish (1551–1860), possibly derives from Bidwell Brook, 'lake' being a local word meaning low lying. The Bidlakes farmed at Westcombe, and in 1670 a family member was churchwarden. The Miller family have probably lived longest in the parish, records showing they were here in 1560. Indeed, the name Myller (it was possibly first spelt with a y) was mentioned in 1555, and descendants still live in the village in 2007. Generations of the Champernownes, who arrived in 1559, lived in the parish for nearly 400 years.

There was no eighteenth-century enclosure movement in Devon to upset matters, and change only began to affect the Devon economy in the nineteenth century, after both the tin and wool trades had declined. The disturbances during and after the Napoleonic Wars may explain why some of the old yeoman families, Bidlakes, Searles and Williams, died out in the middle of the nineteenth century. One branch of the Shinner family, first mentioned in 1666, when Henry Shinner was Vicar of Dartington, also declined.

It was common during the eighteenth century for one branch of a family to be gentry, boasting 'Esq.' after their name, while another pled poverty. Such was the case of the Searles, who were gentry, millers and paupers all at the same time during the latter part of the century. In 1670 there were 18 Searles living in the parish, the name appearing for the last time in 1841.

Phillips, another family name in the village (1579–1882), had four successive generations bearing the Christian name Halse. Halse Phillips, born in 1728, was taught to weave and given a loom by the parish, eventually becoming schoolmaster and parish clerk. He died in 1806.

Many of the Williams family men (1549-1838) were called William Williams.

Early Dartington Family Names

Name	Year	Name	Year
Barret	1813	Nelder	1814
Beer	1814	Niner	1754
Barnes	1760	Osborn	1813
Bidlake	1551	Parnell	1561
Blackler	1634	Phillips	1579
Brimecombe	1820	Putt	1779
Champernowne	1559	Searle	1583
Clear	1756	Shinner	1589
Gidley	1778	Stidston	1589
Gill	1556	Turpin	1828
Gribble	1826	Watson	1713
Hannaford	1664	Webber	1542
Harris	1741	Westerway	1814
Hodge	1713	Whiteway	1724
Irish	1661	Widger	1664
Lapthorn	1614	Williams	1549
Luscombe	1817	Windeatt	1542
Myller/Miller	1555/1560	Morgan	1741
Mugford	1716		

The Poor of Dartington

During 1590/91 an epidemic of Diphtheria swept through the village. Those children who were orphaned were taken in by relatives or friends, while the poorest among the dead were buried at the expense of the parish. In 1602 the first almshouses were founded at Longcause.

The Old Poor Law, passed in 1601 near the end of Queen Elizabeth I's reign, summarised previous legislation and made parishes responsible for their own poor. To cover the cost, a rate was levied on all householders, and overseers were given the duty of distributing the money and recording their outlay. An extract from an order of 1735 , the eighth year of George II's reign, to Arthur Champernowne and Edward Shinner, appointed overseers for the parish of Dartington:

David and Gwen Guy, who were owners of the local shop, c.1920.

Colin and Betty Osborne outside the Village Hall, 25 February 1967.

By virtue of the Statute made (in the Three and Fortieth Year (1601) of the Reign of our late Sovereign Lady Queen Elizabeth) for the Relief of the Poor... That You, together with the Church-wardens... do... take order... for the setting to Work all the Poor within your parish, (as well as married as unmarried) that are able to Work, and have no Means to maintain themselves, nor use nor ordinary and daily Trade of Life to get their Living by and also for the placing out as Apprentices all such Children... whose Parents are not able to... maintain them. And also for the raising of a convenient Stock of Flax, Hemp, Wool, Thread... for that purpose; and also for the providing of necessary relief for all such poor... as are Lame, Old, Blind, Impotent, and unable to Work; wherein if ye be found negligent, or shall fail to meet once a month....then you are to forfeit 20s, a-piece for every month that you shall be found remiss or careless thereigh. And therefore see that you fall not in the Premises at your Perils!

The poor of the parish also benefited through an Act of Parliament designed to protect the wool trade and requiring that the dead, without exception, be buried in a woollen shroud. Failure to comply resulted in a fine, paid by the executors of the will. Parish records state that when, in 1682, Alice Champernowne was buried in linen, the sum of £2.10s.0d. being distributed among 33 poor parishioners. In 1670 Gawing

Champernowne left £20 to be invested for the benefit of the poor in land and, until such land was brought, to be lent out at good security – what happened to the money is not recorded. In 1681 William Bogan left £5.

Appeals for charity were passed on to the parishioners by the Church, usually after a disaster. In 1670 there was an appeal for the captives of the Turks, which raised £7.18s.9d. from 221 parishioners, contributions ranging from 10s. from Edward Champernowne to 1d. from Mary Shinner. Collections in 1677 for the inhabitants of Southwark totalled £1.12s.7d and for Towchester 6s.3d.

Detailed accounts exist in many parishes showing the amount levied and spent on local paupers and on other expenses. For Dartington, the records go back to 1716 and end in August 1836, when 'outdoor relief' (the distribution of money or goods to those in need) was abolished. A detailed record of monthly payments was kept by the 'overseer of the poor' and, by a close study of the documents, it is possible to trace case histories over several years. The same names appear regularly as a residue of people who found it difficult to find employment or maintenance. The recipients often moved up the list in order of length of claim, acquiring 'seniority' as new names were added. There was usually one month a year when two payments were made, one at the beginning and one at the end, making 13 months' payment in all.

Parish records show payments made for teaching those children who were in the care of the parish, the earliest being in 1763: 'Paid to Dame Scagwell for one year's schooling of Wigers boy 4s.' The tuition was probably of low standard, for she was receiving poor relief herself and was buried by the parish when she died the following year. Similar payments appear, mostly for illegitimate children supported by the parish: 'One year's schooling for Gays base child 4s.', 'Elizabeth Gays base child a hat 1s.'.

The following is an extract from the Poor Law accounts for Dartington, dated 11 January, 1799 (the tenth month's pay):

Susanna Cawse	*8s.0d.*
Thomas Kinsman and wife	*£1.0s.0d.*
Elizabeth Stidstone for nursing Huffey	*12s.0d.*
Sarah Lavers	*4s.0d.*
Mary Lavers	*6s.0d.*
Anne Nicholas Child	*4s.0d.*
Mary Searle's Base Child	*4s.0d.*
William Putt in Need	*9s.0d.*
Paid for Schooling James Rulland	*2s.3d.*
Shoemakers Bill	*7s.0d.*
Expense of the Meeting	*1s.0d.*
Paid 2½ County Rates	*£4.17s.6d.*
Paid for Clothing for the Poor	*£2.1s.3d.*

From this can be seen the wide range of local responsibility. A parishioner would be paid for attending to a sick friend, as few hospitals would have been available. Clothing and other provisions would be bought wholesale and kept in the poorhouse or almshouse (as distinct from the 'workhouse', a very different and less charitable institution).

The story of a typical Dartington pauper is that of Anne Nichols (Nicholas), a 22-year-old unmarried parish mother, who gave birth to a daughter on 14 January 1795.

She is first mentioned in the parish Poor Law records in October 1794, when a soldier from Roborough camp, near Plymouth, was sent for after Anne had named him as father of her unborn child; probably the Poor Law officers were trying to establish the parentage of the child to avoid financial liability. In November she received 5s. from the parish funds, probably for warmer clothing for the coming winter.

In early February 1795, Tamsen Miller received 5s. for 'taking' Anne's child to be baptised; at the end of the month, Anne was paid 6s. for her baby's maintenance 'to 6 weeks' – a 'cautious' parish paying its arrears. Payments were then made every month, in several ways, usually: 'Anne Nichols base child' 4s. or 'Anne Nichols in need' – a little extra for necessities she could not afford herself. For these two categories, she received:

	Base child	In need	Total
1794		5s.	5s.
1795	48s.	20s.	68s.
1796	55s.	-	55s.
1797	51s.	3s.	54s.
1798	55s.	-	55s.
1799	54s.	18s.6d.	72s.6d.
1800	51s.	21s.6d.	72s.6d.
1801	55s.	27s.6d.	82s.6d.
1802	55s.	23s.	78s.
1803	35s.	-	35s.

			£28.17s.6d.

Anne did several useful paid parish jobs during these years, which brought her extra money. In October 1797 she was paid 4s. for attending to Jane Lavers, who was confined prior to having an illegitimate child. In May 1798 she received 2s.6d. for the 'stretching' (laying out) of 'the Harris child' and, in February 1801, 2s.6d. for the laying out of Elizabeth Shapter's base child. Additional items supplied to Anne Nichols and paid for by the parish were:

October	*1801*	*Two aprons for her child*	*3s.8d.*
		Pair of shoes for herself	*3s.8d.*
April	*1802*	*A change of clothes*	*4s.8d.*
May		*A 'load of wood'*	*2s.2d.*
October		*Child's shoes*	*8s.1d.*
February	*1803*	*A blanket*	*10s.6d.*
		A gown and aprons	*15s.2d.*
		'8 Fack's of wood'	*4s.4.*
March		*'8 Fack's of wood'*	*4s.4d.*
		One pair of shoes	*3s.10d.*
May		*'A ¼ hundred of wood'*	*6s.9d.*
August		*A pair of shoes*	*4s.3d.*

			£3.7s.5d.

The increase in relief funds during 1802/03 was due to her illness, thus the added: 'in her need' or 'in her sickness'. In January 1802, Anne was given an extra 7s. for ill health, receiving a total of £6.9s.0d. for the year. In August, a member of the parish was paid 5s. to attend to her. From January to September 1803, sickness payments totalled £6.11s.6d., plus 'attendance' fees of £2.7s.0d., including 2s. 'for watching four nights over Anne Nichols'. She died on 16 October 1803, aged 31, cause unknown, though it was possibly from a chill, or consumption, which was common at that time. A parishioner was given 3s. for laying her out and 5s.6d. for watching over the body, while her shroud cost 5s. and the gravedigger received 1s.6d. The cost of the coffin was not entered, but in the November accounts a mysterious 13s.6d. for 'half hundred of wood' is written – six weeks after her death! A total of over £50 (an average of 8s.6d. a month) was given to Anne over a nine-year period – a large sum of money in those days. Perhaps there was certain sympathy for her, given that, as her father was also illegitimate, the parish had become acquainted with the family in previous years. Her orphaned daughter, Anne, aged 8, probably went to live with her grandparents, or was 'apprenticed' out. She was supplied by the parish, as a last act of charity, with a change of clothes at a cost of 5s.6d. Both Anne Nichols' parents outlived her, Mary dying in 1809 and Richard in 1811.

Parish responsibility for the illegitimate children of parishioners was accepted, the child usually being described in the accounts as 'base' or, occasionally, 'bastard'. There might be some scrutiny into such a mother before relief was granted, to ensure that she had in fact been born in the parish – that being the main criterion for payment. After the middle years of the eighteenth century, a negligible illegitimacy rate tended to rise. A rural parish often had a small core of unmarried mothers who, no doubt, brought upon themselves the scorn and bigotry of the local community, until such occurrences became more commonplace. In Dartington, between 1796 and 1802, illegitimate children were born to Mary and Anne Nichols, Mary Searle, Jane Lavers, Elizabeth Shapter, Elizabeth Beaves and Susanna Reeve. The children of Anne Nichols and Mary Searle, were a persistent drain on parish funds over many years. Jane's child was less fortunate – it was born in about September 1797 and died in about July 1799, and the Shapter child died in February 1801, aged about three – infant mortality was high, even in the countryside.

It is impossible to say whether the stationing of soldiers at Dartington during the Napoleonic Wars with France (1793–1815) affected the illegitimacy rate at all. During the wars, there were a number of regiments here: the North Devon Hussars, the Royal Berkshire Regiment and the 3rd, 4th and 9th Dragoon Guards. A soldier was first buried in Dartington (Hall) churchyard in 1797, at which time there was only one 'base' child receiving relief, that of Anne Nichols. Jane Lavers and her child went on relief in December 1797, Mary Searle and child applied in June 1798 and in November 1799, Elizabeth Shapter and child joined them. In May 1801 Elizabeth Beaves' child followed.

The population of Dartington in 1801 was 406. The previous year saw a monthly average of just over 24 claimants of relief, at a cost of almost £120 for the year. This does not include other expenses, such as county rates, etc. The 'total dependants' figure would be approximately double the total number of claimants, perhaps 50 in all, on average, each month in that particular year. If, therefore, about 50 people depended on public charity, that represented about one person in nine or ten, roughly 10 per cent. Most of these people would have either no work or no one to rely on, or would find their earnings insufficient to maintain themselves and, perhaps, a family, too. Some, those 'in need', claimed only occasionally and were not regular recipients. The number of claims usually increased slightly in January, February and March especially, owing to the harsh weather.

The following charges were all too frequent:

Mary Stentiford's coffin	5s.6d.
Paid for stretching Mary Stentiford	3s.
Shroud for Mary Stentiford	3s.
Given to the bearers of Anne Irish in beer and bread	3s.6d.

Food at the funeral was often paid for out of parish funds.

Those whose ability to work was limited were supported by the parish for years on end, often for a large part of their lives.

Amelia (Amy) Weston, born in 1726, died in Dartington poorhouse in 1821, aged 95. She had been on relief since April 1790 (31 years). Her husband died in April 1798. Jane Miller, born in 1764, died in Dartington in January 1837, aged 73. She came 'on the parish' in November 1817. Thus, having lived on charity for 19 years, she died only five months after the abolition of 'outdoor relief' in Dartington in August 1836. Mary Bovey, born in 1761, came on relief in November 1816 and died in Totnes (almost certainly in the workhouse) in 1846, aged 85.

The parish also paid the cost of some 'skilled' medical care for the sick inhabitants, in addition to paying their neighbours to tend them. One parishioner was sent to a 'quack doctor', possibly a specialist, in East Budleigh. Towards the end of the eighteenth century, new methods of offering immunity against epidemics were encouraged: 'Paid Dr. Babbage for Inoculating the Poor (being 49 at 3s.10½d per head) £9.10s.0d.'

The responsibility of the parish seemed all inclusive. It performed, in a limited sense, the function of today's National Health Service and of the government departments regulating labour, education, pensions and national insurance, as well as that of Job Centre. It maintained its roads and provided 'national assistance' for the poor – shelter, food, clothing and basic necessities. By the early-nineteenth century, the expense of the Poor Law system was rising fast, especially after the Napoleonic Wars, when unemployment increased.

In 1818, £8million was distributed to the poor nationally, a record amount. In Dartington, payments were fairly steady until about the 1790s, when there were variations due to bad harvests – the availability of cheap bread meant a decline in the distribution of poor relief. The years 1790–95 showed a steep climb, which tailed off until relief rocketed in the years of scarcity during the war, the price of corn reflecting Britain's economic isolation from the continent. The figures fell in the immediate postwar years, despite the Corn Law of 1815, which prohibited imports of foreign grain until British corn reached 80s. per quarter, then rose from 1830 until the abolition of poor relief in 1836.

The Poor Law Amendment Act of 1834 grouped parishes into 'unions', with a central workhouse where conditions were made deliberately harsh. Demands for a change in the system were reinforced by the growing spirit of self-reliance in an England of increasing industrialism and prosperity. Outdoor relief was abolished and the outlay on the poor, including the old and the sick, fell rapidly – at what

human cost we do not know. There were obvious deficiencies in the old system. The 'deterrent' element had declined by the eighteenth century and the 'cushioning' effects had grown. Perhaps it was indeed 'a bounty on indolence and vice', as the Poor Law Commissioners maintained, but between 1834 and about 1909 onwards, there was a gap when the aged and the sick had virtually no provision made for them and the shadow of the workhouse lay across their lives.

Overseers of the Poor
Miscellaneous Papers

1658	John Tucker. Bond in £5
1673	John Stuart, weaver, and Gertrude his wife. Certificate of Settlement in Staverton.
1675	Mary Rogers, daughter of John Rogers of Dodbrooke, millar. Certificate of Settlement in Dodbrooke 1675.
1681	Jane Hannaford. Certificate of Settlement in South Brent.
1682	Joan Algar, widow. Certificate of Settlement in Ermington.
1683	Edward Williams, his wife and child. Certificate of Settlement in Rattery.
1683-1685	Frisett Chase. Settlement in Bovey Tracey (relative sessions papers 1683–850).
1685	Agnes Holl, spinster. Certificate in (Church) Stanton, Devon.
1685	Henry Netherton. Certificate of Settlement in North Petherwin.
1685	Ann Stevens wanting to live with her uncle, George Blackaller of Dartington: Certificate of Settlement in Highweek.
1687	Elizabeth Tucker, single woman, pregnant: removal to Exeter, St Mary Major.
1690	John Gill, yeoman, and Agnes Gill. Bond in 10 shillings and 6 pence.
1704	Joseph Barns, Grace his wife, Joan and Joseph children, removal to Rattery.
1704	John Chase, Mary his wife and their four children, removal to Berry Pomeroy.
1706	Grace Tucker, single woman who died in child bed.
1707	Honor Oliver, single woman, Nicholas Preston, yeoman, father of her male bastard – pay £1.1 shilling per week.
1708	Robert Bunclark, weaver, Joanna his wife and Thomas and Sarah their children. Certificate of Settlement in Broadhempston.
1718	John Askecott, weaver, removal to Newberry, Berkshire.
1721	James Reeves, Agnes his wife and John their child. Certificate of Settlement in North Huish.
1722	John Blight now in North Huish – born in South Brent – apprenticed there to Henry Farley when he was 13. His master died, he went to Dartington and apprenticed himself to William Gidley. When he was 20 his Masters Trade failed, he gave a guinea to the rest of his apprenticeship and he went to work in South Brent, by the week for 9 weeks. Then went to Diptford and served Mr Hole for a year except 8 or 9 days, then to Dean Prior for 6 months, then to North Huish, after 5 months he married, he was about 23 and has worked by the day since.
1725	Grace Terry. Edward Langman of Totnes, father of her female bastard, born 5 June 1725: to pay 7s. and 1s.6d. per week.
1731	John Tremlett, Innholder and Joan his wife. Certificate of Settlement in Totnes.
1748	Richard Andrew, Excise Officer and George Hayman, paper maker. Bound in £20 for maintenance of Mary Hallett's unborn bastard.
1769	John Ward, yeoman, father of Mary Gill's male bastard, born at Forder on 4 April 1769.
1777	Henrietta Gill, removal to Exeter, St Peter's (The Close).
1777	Agnes Weston, single woman. John Grant of Diptford, husbandman, father of her female bastard, born August, to pay 1s. per week.
1778	Jane Harris otherwise Mitchell: William Faremouth, father of her female bastard, born 15 June 1778, to pay £1.13.6d per week.
1783	Ann Harris otherwise Mitchell: single woman and her male bastard, removal to Dittisham.
1794	Richard Cumming, now in Dartington. Born in South Brent and apprenticed there until 24, when he was 21 his master let him go, but employed him as a yearly servant for about 9 months.

He then came to Dartington, spent a month as a day labourer and got married.

1794   *Ann Nichols, single woman. James Plant of Roborough Camp Militia, man is father of her unborn bastard.*

1795   *Mary Binmore, single woman. Now in Dean Prior, born in Buckfastleigh, she was apprenticed to John Hewitt of Dean Prior, afterwards she went to South Brent as a servant for one year with Richard Austin, returned to Dean Prior for a year with Thomas Hunt, then to Dartington as a weekly servant with Thomas Tucker for 1 year 9 months and then went back to Dean Prior.*

1798   *Mary Searle, single. Richard Plan a Private in the Surrey Light Horse, is father of her female bastard, born 28 March 1798.*

1806   *Elizabeth Stidstone, single woman. Andrew Tozer an apprentice to Mr Bidlake, father of her unborn bastard.*

1808   *Richard Webber, a poor child to be apprenticed in Dartington. Certificate of Settlement in Staverton.*

1810   *Thomas Taverner, now in Dartington, born in Broadwoodwidger, soon after they moved to Germansweek, where his father had a freehold estate until he was about 20, since then he has worked in various places, 2 weeks ago he married in Tavistock.*

1813   *Mary Phillips: Henry Searle, labourer, father of her male bastard born 3 June at Westcombe, to pay 9s. and 2s. per week.*

1814   *William Rapsney, son of William Rapsney, a soldier in His Majesty's 77th Regiment of Foot. Mary Guskott in Rattery, now with Susan Williams, Nr Staverton Bridge, Dartington and is pregnant.*

1815   *George Crout, now in Dartington, born in Sampford Courtenay, when he was 7 he was apprenticed there to John Lethbridge, yeoman, when he was 10 left his master without consent and went to live with Henry Hamlyn, yeoman, in Broadwoodwidger for 7 years, he went to live with Richard Croute in Bishopsteignton and stayed about 2 years, he then returned to Henry Hamlyn for a year and then 2 further years, he was over 22 years old, he then went to Daniel Badcock, yeoman in Lifton, after 7 months he went to John Strong in Whitchurch by the year, after 6 months he married and lived in a house belonging to Mr Strong, paying no rent and working for him as a labourer.*

1815   *Agnes Plaice removal to Stoke Damerell.*

1815   *Mary Huford removal to Totnes.*

1815   *Ann Irish, now Ann Collings. Richard Hodge, yeoman, father of her male bastard.*

1815   *Henry Putt, labourer, born in Dartington. When he was 9 apprenticed to Andrew Niner there, after 2 years his Master died, but he stayed with his widow Mary for 5 years. He was 16 when he was assigned to John Damwal of Harberton, after 2 years his Master died and he spent another year with Mr Symonds there. He served as a weekly servant with Richard Hamlyn of South Brent for 9 months, then 7 months with Samuel Faremouth of Dartington and then lodged 2 months in Dartington and then worked for Samuel Faremouth again.*

1816   *George Hannaford now in Dartington, born there. When 9 he was apprenticed to Robert Wills, to learn tailoring in Dartmouth. He does not know which Parish, believes that the Indenture was drawn up by Timmings, a Romish Priest living with Edward Cary Esq. of Totnes and that Mr Cary paid 10 guineas to Richard Wills. After 20 months he ran away and returned to Dartington where he worked as a carpenter for his father, then lived with Mrs Edwards in Totnes for 7 or 8 months. He was then apprenticed by Dartington to Mr Niner of Allerton, where he stayed until he was 20 when he joined a Regiment of Dragoons, from which he was discharged in 1814.*

1816   *Robert Hannaford, born in Rattery. Apprenticed to George Gidley when he was 9 and served his time. Then worked as a labourer in Dartington for 3 months, he then lived in Rattery and worked as a labourer in Dartington for 6 months, Rattery for 2 months, Dartington for 12 months, got married and has lived and worked in Dartington ever since.*

1816   *Thomas Farley now in Dartington, born in Totnes, when he was 11 he was apprenticed, with his mother's consent, to John Bowden of Staverton, yeoman, and stayed with him for 8 years 9 months, when his master died, he came to Dartington and lived with Mary Viner for a month, then went to Totnes for 6 months, got married and came back to Dartington and has worked as a labourer since.*

1816   *Richard King, labourer, has abandoned his wife and child in Dartington: warrant for arrest for non-payment of maintenance.*

1816   *Thomas Morgan, now in Dartington, born in Brent (? South), when he was 8 apprenticed by Diptford to George Perrot of North Huish, served his time and then stayed for 3 months, after which he went to Harberton and worked as a weekly labourer for Thomas Weymouth, yeoman, for 9 weeks, then Thomas Leer as a daily labourer for 3 years, he then went to sea for 3 years and 10 months and was discharged, returned to Thomas Leer for a year, then moved to Dartington and worked as a day labourer for John Searle, yeoman.*

1816   *Alexander Mullis now in Dartington, born in Harberton. When he was 8 apprenticed there to Richard Perring, yeoman, for East Lee estate. When he was 18 his master moved to Slapton and he stayed with his father without consent at 4s. a week, he got married and worked as a labourer with his father on the roads for 12 months, then went to work in Dartington for 2 years, then lived and worked here for 4 years.*

1816   *Francis Parnell, wife of Giles Parnell, a seaman, now in New Foundland, and Mary Ann daughter age 5: Removal from Totnes.*

1816   *Thomas Harrison, now in Dartington, born there. When he was 6¹/₂ years was apprenticed to Thomas Ward there. Lived with him for 13¹/₂ years, went to Topsham for 11¹/₂ months and returned to Thomas Ward for 2 weeks when his time ran out. He then lived with parents and worked as a labourer for 9 months. Went to Torbryan as a weekly servant for 16 months. He then got married and moved to Totnes, where he rented a house for £3.10s and worked as day labourer.*

1816   *Thomas Osburn, now in Dartington, born in Chagford, when he was 6¹/₂ years was apprenticed there to Gilbert Scot. After his apprenticeship, went to Broadhempston and lived with Thomas Palk for a year. He then went to Dartington as a servant to Thomas Skinner for 6 months. He then went to Newfoundland for 3 years and then returned to Thomas Skinner for 9 months. He got married and went to Staverton for a year and rented a house for £1.1s. He then spent 4 years in Rattery, rent free. Then came back to Dartington, renting at £1.10s.*

1816   *Elizabeth Phillips, born in Dartington and apprenticed there to Mr Jackson of Hood, after this she worked for him as a servant for 5 more years. She then married and went to Totnes for a year, during which time she had a child and her husband died. She went back to Dartington and had another child. After her children were apprenticed, she lived with Mr Seattle of Allerton, Dartington for 2¹/₂ years, then 5 months with Mr Brown in Harberton, she then hired herself to Mrs Bental in Totnes as a servant for nearly 2 years, came back to Dartington and then to Mr Hicks of Broadhempston by the week, returning briefly to Dartington and then back to Mr Hicks for 7 months, back to Dartington for 5 months and then to Brixham for 9 months.*

1816   *Christopher Searle, now in Dartington, born there, lived with his parents until he was 8 years old was then apprenticed to Edmund Moan of Harberton for Pelow in Dartington. Finished his apprenticeship and served a further year. He married and lived and worked as a labourer for 18 years in Totnes and has been in Dartington for 2 months.*

1816   *James Stephens, now in Dartington, born in Rattery and lived there with his parents until he was 20 years. His father renting an estate for £15 a year. He then lived with his brother in Rattery for 6 months. Then got married and lived in Rattery, but worked as a labourer in Dartington for 3 years. Then lived in Totnes and worked in Rattery for 2 years, and then lived in Dartington and worked as a labourer in Rattery.*

1816   *Thomas Stidston, labourer, now in Dartington, born in South Brent. Lived there with his parents until he was 7 years, then he was apprenticed to John Partridge of East Allington, yeoman. His uncle, where he lived until he was 20, when his Master gave up, but got him a place with John Watson of Dartington, with whom he lived as a servant for a year, during which time his time expired. He then went to live with William Hudder of North Huish, yeoman, for 13 months. Went to London, living with his father, for a while, returned to Devon and worked for himself as a labourer. Went to his Uncle William Turpin, who lived in Blakewill in Diptford, while there he was taken ill and relieved by North Huish. He then volunteered in the South Devon Militia for 14 years – got married in Dartington – then got a substitute and returned to Dartington and has worked as a labourer there ever since.*

1816   *William Webber, now in Dartington, born there and lived with his parents until he was 8, when he was apprenticed to John Watson there. When he finished his apprenticeship he went to live with Edward Parnell, yeoman, in Rattery for a year, he agreed for another year, but only stayed 3 months, he then volunteered in the East Devon Militia, where he served for 4 years 11 months and 5 days. While in the Militia he got married, when he left he lived in Rattery and worked as a labourer in Dartington.*

1818	*Joseph Bond, a prisoner in the Bridwell, Warrant for arrest: Maintenance for Mary Carter's base child.*
1818	*Mary Carter, expenses connected with her female bastard.*
1819	*Joseph Creese, a vagrant: Removed from Exeter St. Paul.*
1819-20	*James Denley, mason. Now in Dartington, born in Chudleigh, lived with his parents until he was 6½, when he was apprenticed to Mr William Luscombe of Bickington, after 3 years his master moved to Broadhempston and served 6 years, then John Dodd was committed for felony and he came to Dartington and lived with his former master for 4 months, then he went to Totnes for 6 months, then South Brent for 6 months. Exeter for 3 weeks, married and came back to Dartington.*
1820	*John Faremouth junr, now in Dartington, born there and rented there at £140pa for 10 years, he quit in 1819 and spent 6 months in Kenn.*
1820	*Jane Shapter, single woman, now in Dartington, born in Buckfastleigh, apprenticed there to Philip Luscombe of Wotton. After her apprenticeship, she lived for 4 years with her mother in Buckfastleigh and then hired herself to Mr Vinney of Broadhempston for 3 months, then lived with her mother at Baddeford for 3 and 4 months. Then hired herself to Mr William Bowden of Burnstone in Staverton by the month for 2 years and one month, then with Mr Edwards of Riverford, Staverton, for 4½ years by the month. Then with Mr Hawkins of Newtake, Staverton, by the month for 3 years. She left him 2 years ago, she then lived with various people for 1 year and then hired herself to Mr Vinney of Broadhempston by the week, she left him 5 weeks ago, then spent 3 weeks with Mary Guskott in Rattery. She is now with Susan Williams near Staverton Bridge in Dartington and is pregnant.*
1821	*Marenea Hicks, single woman. Removal from Stoke Damerall. Endorsed: unable to be removed due to sickness.*
1821	*William Hollet and Elizabeth, 14, his daughter. Removal from Exeter St Mary Major.*
1822	*Rebecca Barns: Andrew Miller father of her female bastard, born 11 November 1822: to pay £1.10s.6d per week.*
1822	*George Gill, blacksmith, now in Dartington and born there. He lived with his parents until he was 15, when he was privately apprenticed to Joseph Newman of Churston Ferrers. After 3 years his Master failed and by consent his Indentures were destroyed and he returned to his father in Dartington. After a year he went as a servant to Philip Furnish in Harberton for 9 months, then to (blank) Barton in Buckfastleigh for 8 months, by the week. He then went to Newfoundland for 4 years and then got married.*
1822	*John Jackson, now in Dartington, born in Rattery, where his parents were settled with them there until he was 5, when they moved to Harberton, where he lived with them for 7 years. He then hired himself as an apprentice to Richard Watson, there for 7 years, but without Indenture. He then went to Newfound for a year and on his return, spent 2 months in Harberton as a lodger and then got married. He moved to Dartington and rented a house for £3 per annum.*
1822	*Samuel Searle, now in Dartington, he was born there, but his parents were settled in South Brent. When he was 10 years he was apprenticed to Mr Foal of South Brent. After 8 years went with his masters to Harberton for 2 months. Then his masters told him to go and find a place as a servant, so about 4 years ago he hired himself to Mr Moysey of Dartington as a weekly servant and stayed 8 weeks, there was 4 months of his apprenticeship, he then worked as a carter with Mr Chaffe in Rattery until his apprenticeship ended, he then stayed for 15 months as a weekly servant.*
1822	*Samuel Searle and Margaret his wife with Joseph and John their children, removal to South Brent.*
1822	*Richard Trimble. Now in Stokeinteignhead, born in Denbury, when he was 7½ he was apprenticed there to Richard Trull, after 2 years he was assigned to Robert Terry of Torbryan, where he lived for 1½ years, his master then moved to Harberton for 6½ years, then to Dartington where he finished his term, he then worked for him for 2 years as a weekly servant. He then hired himself to Joseph Trull of Stokeinteignhead by the week for a year and 10 weeks, then served one month in the Devon Militia and returned to Mr Trull and finished the year, he then agreed with Mr Trull as a monthly servant and served 10 months, he then went to Robert Symons in Harberton by the week and then went back to Mr Trull in Stokeinteignhead as a weekly servant for 3 months, he then got married in Stokenham.*
1822	*John Wakeham: Removal from Ugborough.*
	Elizabeth his wife endorsed – too sick to be removed: 9 October '22.
	Endorsed: Elizabeth is recovered by 19 March 1823.
1822	*John Waycott. Now in Dartington, born in Totnes, but his parents were settled in Staverton,*

lived in Totnes until he was 4 when they moved to Staverton, lived with his parents until 14 and then as a lodger until 18, he then went to Ashprington and lived as a lodger with his father for 4 years, then went to sea for 10 months, came to Dartington where he has lived for 9 months and has got married.

1822	*Jonas Williams, Mary his wife and Richard 4 months their child: Removal from Totnes.*
1823	*Richard Honeywell, labourer, and Maria his wife: Removal to Harberton (File).*
1823	*Mary Hodge discharge from Thomas Lear, as he has not fed or clothed her.*
1826	*Robert Collins, Mary his wife, and Mary Grace 4, Robert 2½ years their children removal.*
1827	*Thomas Adams and Mary his wife: Removal to Charleton.*
1827	*Richard Hodge, yeoman, father of Ann Irish's male bastard with list of expenses.*
1827	*Thomas Stidstone and wife Elizabeth: Removal to North Huish.*
1829	*John Hannaford: Removal to Bovey Tracey.*
1830	*James Brimicombe, labourer. Now in Dartington, born in Stoke Gabriel, he lived there with his parents until he was 7 when he was apprenticed to Mr Nicholas Moysey, when he was 19½ he went with his master to Dartington, when his apprenticeship finished he worked as a weekly servant to Mr John Huxham of Harberton for 6 months, then he lived as a lodger in Stoke Gabriel for 2 months, he then worked for Mr Robert Hodge there for a month and then a year and then another, but left after 6 months and went to Marldon and served several masters there, he married in Ipplepen.*
1832	*Thomas Stoneman, now in Tormoham, born in North Tawton. When he was 11 he was apprenticed there to Mr John Brock of Stone, a farmer. When he was 19 he ran away and worked for Mr Tucker of Kingsteignton for a week, then Mr Preston in Whitestone for 1 month, Mr Jarmin in Bickleigh for 5 months, Mr Reeve at Exwick Barton for 3 months, Mr Broomhead of West Teignmouth for 8 months, Mr Roebuck in East Teignmouth for 5 months, left him for a month by request, then went back to him. He then married Thomasine in Dartington and lives in Tormoham.*
1833	*Maria Stephens: Removal to Buckland Monachorum.*
1835	*John Clear, Verdict of suicide and order for burial in the churchyard.*
1846	*Jane Brimicombe, a pauper and Charles her son 3 months: Removal to Stoke Gabriel (File).*

The Marriage Act of 1755

In 1755 Lord Hardwicke's Marriage Act laid down that marriages should be registered in a prescribed form and that the entries should be signed by both husband and wife. Those who could not write were to make their mark (x). By analysing the entries in the marriage register, it is possible to calculate roughly the degree of illiteracy prevalent in the parish at any given time. In the five years immediately after the legislation the space for signatures has usually been filled in by the parson, and very few actual signatures or 'marks' appear.

The graph shows a reasonably downward trend in the number of illiterates, and at most times the percentage of illiterate women exceeds that of men. The marked drop in male illiteracy between 1790 and 1810 may have been due to the teaching ability of Halse Phillips, who appears to have been the village schoolmaster for some years in the 1770s and 1780s.

Records of educational activities in the village during this period are few.

The approximate percentage of parishioners making 'marks' (x)

	Men (per cent)	Women (per cent)
1760–65:	65	50
1765–70:	70	70
1770–75:	64	83
1775–80:	60	64
1780–85:	42	79
1785–90:	49	42
1790–95:	30	43
1795–1800:	35	52
1800–05:	30	59
1805–10:	21	41
1810–15:	49	53
1815–20:	42	38
1820–25:	49	49
1825–30:	11	31
1830–35:	21	24
1835–40:	38	41
1840–45:	22	21
1845–50:	3	48

CHAPTER 2

Early Days: Marriages, Births, Baptisms and the Regiments at Barracks Hill

Extracts from the Parish Records
of Early Marriages at Dartington Hall Church

25 February	1589	*Thomas Shinner and Mary Martin: both of this Parish.*
8 September	1737	*Richard Mayford (East Ogwell) and Mary Caws (Dartington)*
6 November	1737	*George Maddicks (Totnes) and Elizabeth Bully (Denbury)*
9 January	1738	*John Blackler and Mary Glarris: both of this Parish.*
26 March	1738	*Nicholas Constable and Elizabeth Hutchings.*
21 April	1741	*John Bidlake and Charity Barons.*
19 May	1741	*William Soper (Harberton) and Mary Widdecombe.*
29 May	1741	*John Morgan and Joan Yabbycombe.*
4 April	1743	*John Hannaford and Ann Neatherton: both of this Parish.*
28 October	1743	*Peter Lose and Mary Evens.*
6 November	1743	*Dorothy Bidlake and John Wills (Totnes).*
30 April	1745	*John Shinner and Wilmet Burt: both of Dartington.*
8 May	1750	*John Baker and Joan Phillips: both of Dartington.*
31 March	1752	*Thomas Shinner and Rachael Harris: both of Dartington.*
3 April	1752	*John Favenmouth and Mary Pulling.*
10 April	1752	*Thomas Ward and Elizabeth Searle.*
10 October	1752	*William Favenmouth and Mary Baker.*
3 March	1754	*John Niner (Mariner) and Margaret Bidlake.*

St Mary's Church, Dartington, in 1930.

Births Registered at Dartington 1778–1789

1778	11 February	Peggy, daughter of Christopher and Grace Bidlake.
	27 February	Christopher Watson, son of John and Mary Helms.
	21 May	Christopher, son of Andrew and Mary Watson.
	15 June	Jane, daughter/base child of Jane Harris.
	28 June	Mary, daughter of William and Susannah Gidley.
	28 August	Hannah, daughter of Humphrey and Joan Watson.
	11 December	Mary, daughter of Peter and Mary Clear.
1779	10 May	Peggy, daughter/base child of Margaret Shinner.
	23 August	Mary, daughter of William and Mary Faremouth.
	31August	Mary, daughter of William and Mary Hannaford.
	6 September	Robert, son of Robert and Sarah Helms.
	15 November	Betsey, daughter of Christopher and Grace Bidlake.
	26 December	William, son of William and Dinah Putt.
1780	14 January	John, son of Christopher and Agnes Niner.
	16 January	Humphrey, son of John and Sarah Watson.
	11 February	Andrew, son of Andrew and Mary Watson.
	15 August	Mary, daughter of William (Junr) and Mary Faremouth.
	17 September	Joanna, daughter of Peter and Mary Clear.
	26 September	Mary daughter of John (Junr) and Mary Faremouth.
	16 October	Wilmot, daughter of Humphrey and Hannah Watson.
1781	15 March	Nancy, daughter of Andrew and Mary Watson.
	17 March	Christopher, son of Christopher and Grace Bidlake.
	8 April	Mary, daughter/base child of Mary Bronvic.
	9 May	Christopher, son of Christopher and Agnes Niner.
	10 July	John, son of John and Susanna Petherbridge.
	5 August	John, son of John and Ann Penny.
	12 August	John, son of Richard and Joan Ralland.
	28 October	Richard, son of Solomon and Mary Collins.
	7 November	George, son of George and Susanna Franks.
	24 December	William, son of Richard and Elizabeth Mugford.
1782	27 January	Grace, daughter of John and Mary Faremouth.
	25 February	Nicholas, son of Joseph and Mary Barnes.
	10 April	Elizabeth, daughter of Humphrey and Joan Watson.
	16 April	John, son of William and Margaret Hollett.
	7 July	John, son/base child of Mary Harris.
	23 September	Elizabeth, daughter of William and Mary Hannaford.
1783	20 January	John, son of Christopher and Grace Bidlake.
	4 March	Andrew, son of Christopher and Agnes Niner.
	10 March	Edward, son of John and Ann Penny.
	16 April	William, son of John and Grace Blight.
	3 May	John, son of Thomas and Elizabeth Rimes.
	19 May	Mary, daughter of William and Dinah Putt.
	29 June	John, son of John and Francis Searle.
1784	19 February	Mary, daughter of Humphrey and Joan Watson.
	15 March	James, son of John and Susanna Petherbridge.
	2 April	William, son of James and Elizabeth Hurford.
	7 July	Mary, daughter of William and Margaret Hollett.
	24 August	Samuel, son of Samuel and Ann Penny.
	25 August	Susan, daughter of Christopher and Grace Bidlake.

	27 September	William, son of William and Mary Parnell.
	30 September	Agnes, daughter of Christopher and Agnes Niner.
	14 October	John James, son of the Revd John Ameyatt (South Brent) and his wife Margaret.
	12 November	Grace, daughter of Richard and Elizabeth Mugford.
	25 November	Frances, daughter of John and Frances Searle.
	25 November	Mary, daughter of John and Mary Widdicombe.
1785	11 February	Ann Cawse, daughter of John and Ann Penny.
	21 February	Philip, son of Philip and Agnes Rockey.
	27 February	Joseph, son of John and Thomasine Yeoman.
	11 March	Margaret, daughter/base child of Jane Mitchell.
	17 March	John, son of John (Junr) and Mary Faremouth.
	17 March	Christopher Elms, son/base child of Mary, wife of John Godfree.
1786	4 January	David, son of John and Grace Blight.
	30 January	George, son of Valentine and Hannah Hannaford.
	11 February	Edward, son of John and Elizabeth Parnell.
	29 March	Thomas, son of Humphrey and Joan Watson.
	28 May	Margaret, daughter of Richard and Mary Nichols.
	28 May	James, son of Christopher and Agnes Niner.
	11 June	John, son of John and Sarah Harris.
	19 June	James, son of Christopher and Grace Bidlake.
	20 July	Elizabeth, daughter of John and Frances Searle.
	2 August	William, son of John and Mary Widdicombe.
	24 December	John, son of Richard and Rebecca Trist.
1787	9 January	Jenney, daughter of John (Junr) and Joan Bidlake.
	28 January	Elizabeth, daughter of James and Elizabeth Hurford.
	29 January	Mary, daughter of John and Mary Bovey.
	15 March	Peter, son of Thomas and Elizabeth Rimes.
	19 March	William, son of Gregory and Elizabeth Webber.
	2 April	Mary, daughter of Richard and Mary Cumming.
	27 April	John, son of William and Margaret Hollett.
	20 May	Thomas, son/base child of Grace Marsh.
	20 May	Giles, son of William and Mary Parnell.
	5 June	Mary, daughter of John and Frances Searle.
	5 June	John Lavis, son of John and Sarah Harris.
	17 June	John, son of Giles and Ann Shinner.
	19 October	Mary, daughter of Samuel and Ann Penny.
	3 December	Richard, son of Richard and Honor Heath.
	10 December	Elizabeth, daughter of John and Charity Rogers (Totnes).
	23 December	Elizabeth, daughter of Peter and Mary Clear.
1788	6 January	Arthur, son of Richard and Joan Smerdon.
	30 January	John, son of Valentine and Hannah Hannaford.
	2 February	Mary, daughter/base child of Mary Nichols.
	5 March	Richard Baker, son of Christopher and Agnes Niner.
	29 April	Richard, son of John and Grace Blight.
	16 July	Rebecca Shinner, daughter of Richard and Rebecca Trist.
	19 July	Francis Garde, son of John and Frances Searle.
	18 August	William, son of Matthew and Mary Foall.
	4 September	Richard, son of Richard and Elizabeth Mugford.
	10 October	John, son of John and Mary Widdecombe.
	3 November	Mary, daughter of John (Junr) and Joan Mitchell.
	8 December	Agnes, daughter of William and Mary Hannaford.
	10 December	John Palfrey, son of John and Joanna Baker.
	10 December	Mary, daughter of Giles and Ann Shinner.

	14 December	Wilmot, daughter of Andrew and Mary Watson.
	26 December	John, son of Philip and Elizabeth Shapter.
1789	26 February	Susan, daughter of John and Susanna Petherbridge.
	26 March	Thomas, son of John and Sarah Harris.
	14 April	Thomas Atwill, son of John and Sarah Watson.
	9 May	William, son of George (Junr) and Ann Penny.
	10 May	Robert Watson, son of John and Mary Faremouth.
	14 June	William, son of William and Margaret Hollett.
	22 June	Nancy, daughter of John and Mary Godfree.
	6 July	William, son of Thomas and Elizabeth Rimes.
	23 July	John, son of Humphrey and Joan Watson.

Baptisms Recorded from 1555 to 1840

1555	5 December	Luccy Myller, daughter of Thomas Myller.
1556	January	June Gill, daughter of John Gill.
1664	14 January	Cornealus, son of William and Margaret Hannaford.
	24 January	Richard, son of Thomas and Agnes Miller.
	26 July	Ann and Mary, daughters of Edward and Henretta Shinner.
	4 December	Ann, daughter of Benjimin Widger.
1684	19 June	Henry, son of Henry and Margaret Champernowne.
1694	18 January	Richard, son of John and Grace Gill.
1711	May	Francis, son of Arthur and Elguire Champernowne.
1739	11 January	Nancy, daughter of Henry and Alice Gill.
1740	15 March	Mary, daughter of Ballentine and Patience Hannaford.
1753	10 April	Anne, daughter of John and Wilmot Shinner.
	26 August	Agnes, daughter of John and Joan Weston.
	7 November	Elizabeth, daughter of Thomas and Thomasine Miller.
	2 December	Mary, daughter of John and Ann Hannaford.
1754	1 January	Thomas, son of William and Elizabeth Searle.
	13 March	John, son of James and Ann Bidlake.
	21 October	Andrew, son of John and Margaret Millner.
1755	21 February	John, son of John and Wilmot Shinner.
1756	4 May	Mary, daughter of Thomas and Thomasine Miller.
1757	9 May	Wilmot, daughter of John and Wilmot Shinner.
	9 May	Jane, daughter of Olaffe and Jane Phillips.
	12 June	Thomas, son/base child of Agnes Phillips.
1778	1 March	Peggy, daughter of Christopher and Grace Bidlake.
	4 March	Thomas, son/base child of Agnes Watson.
	7 March	Ann, daughter of Nicholas and Ann Hannaford.
	15 March	Christopher Watson, son of John and Mary Helms.
	7 June	Christopher, son of Andrew and Mary Watson.
	28 June	Jane, daughter/base child of Jane Harris.
	5 July	Mary, daughter of William and Susannah Gidley.

	18 August	John, son/base child of Joan Phillips.
	23 September	Hannah, daughter of Humphrey and Joan Watson.
	20 October	John, son of John and Ann Williams.
1779	7 January	Mary, daughter of Peter and Mary Clear.
	20 June	Peggy, daughter/base child of Margaret Shinner.
	5 September	Mary, daughter of William and Mary Faremouth.
	19 September	Mary, daughter of William and Mary Hannaford.
	26 September	Robert, son of Robert and Sarah Helms.
	9 December	Betsey, daughter of Christopher and Grace Bidlake.
1780	9 January	William, son of William and Dinah Putt.
	2 February	Humphrey, son of John and Sarah Watson.
	8 February	John, son of Christopher and Agnes Niner.
	8 March	Andrew, son of Andrew and Mary Watson.
	18 August	Mary, daughter of William (Junr) and Mary Faremouth.
	29 September	Mary, daughter of John (Junr) and Mary Faremouth.
	8 October	Joanna, daughter of Peter and Mary Clear.
	12 November	Wilmot, daughter of Humphrey and Hannah Watson.
1781	11 April	Nancy, daughter of Andrew and Mary Watson.
	11 April	Christopher, son of Christopher and Grace Bidlake.
	22 April	Mary, daughter/base child of Mary Bronvic.
	30 May	Christopher, son of Christopher and Agnes Niner.
	26 July	John, son of John and Susanna Petherbridge.
	21 August	John, son of Richard and Joan Ralland.
	26 August	John, son of John and Ann Penny.
	11 November	Richard, son of Solomon and Mary Collins.
	25 November	George, son of George and Susanna Franks.
	28 November	William, son of John and Margaret Niner.
	2 December	Robert, son of John and Sarah Watson.
1782	6 January	William, son of Richard and Elizabeth Mugford.
	20 February	Grace, daughter of John and Mary Faremouth.
	10 March	Nicholas, son of Joseph and Mary Barnes.
	5 May	Elizabeth, daughter of Humphrey and Joan Watson.
	12 May	John, son of William and Margaret Hollet.
	11 August	John, son/base child of Mary Harris.
	6 October	Elizabeth, daughter of William and Mary Hannaford.
1783	20 January	John, son of Christopher and Grace Bidlake.
	26 March	Andrew, son of Christopher and Agnes Niner.
	3 April	Edward, son of John and Ann Penny.
	4 May	William, son of John and Grace Blight.
	10 May	John, son of Thomas and Elizabeth Rimes.
	30 May	Mary, daughter of William and Dina Putt.
	30 June	John, son of John and Frances Searle.
1784	14 March	Mary, daughter of Humphrey and Joan Watson.
	27 March	James, son of John and Susanna Peterbridge.
	15 April	William, son of James and Elizabeth Hurford.
	25 July	Mary, daughter of William and Margaret Hollet.
	25 September	Susan, daughter of Christopher and Grace Bidlake.
	28 September	Samuel, son of Samuel and Ann Penny.
	10 October	William, son of William and Mary Parnell.
	15 October	John James, son of Revd John Ameyatt (South Brent) and his wife Margaret.
	21 October	Agnes, daughter of Christopher and Agnes Niner.

	26 November	*Frances, daughter of John and Frances Searle.*
	12 December	*Grace, daughter of Richard and Elizabeth Mugford.*
	22 December	*Mary, daughter of John and Mary Widdicombe.*
1785	19 March	*Ann Cawse, daughter of John and Ann Penny.*
	20 March	*Philip, son of Philip and Agnes Rockey.*
	27 March	*Joseph, son of John and Thomasine Yeaman.*
	11 April	*Margaret, daughter/base child of Jane Mitchell.*
	14 April	*John, son of John (Junr) and Mary Faremouth.*
	17 April	*Christopher Elms, son/base child of Mary, wife of John Godfree.*
1786	22 January	*David, son of John and Grace Blight.*
	26 January	*Edward, son of John and Elizabeth Parnell.*
	2 March	*George, son of Valentine and Hannah Hannaford.*
	19 April	*Thomas, son of Humphrey and Joan Watson.*
	11 June	*John, son of John and Sarah Harris.*
	11 June	*Margaret, daughter of Richard and Mary Nichols.*
	19 June	*James, son of Christopher and Grace Bidlake.*
	20 June	*James, son of Christopher and Agnes Niner.*
	21 July	*Elizabeth, daughter of John and Frances Searle.*
	13 September	*William, son of John and Mary Widdicombe.*
1787	24 January	*John, son of Richard and Rebecca Trist.*
	9 February	*Jenney, daughter of John Michell (Junr) and Joan Bidlake.*
	11 February	*Elizabeth, daughter of James and Elizabeth Hurford.*
	11 February	*Mary, daughter of John and Mary Bovey.*
	5 April	*William, son of Gregory and Elizabeth Webber.*
	11 April	*Peter, son of Thomas and Elizabeth Rimes.*
	22 April	*Mary, daughter of Richard and Mary Cumming.*
	22 May	*John, son of William and Margaret Hollett.*
	1 June	*Thomas, son/base child of Grace Marsh.*
	8 June	*Giles, son of William and Mary Parnell.*
	10 June	*Mary, daughter of John and Frances Searle.*
	24 June	*John Lavis, son of John and Sarah Harris.*
	10 July	*John, son of Giles and Ann Shinner.*
	20 November	*Mary, daughter of Samuel and Ann Penney.*
	18 December	*Richard, son of Richard and Honor Heath.*
1788	2 January	*Elizabeth, daughter of John and Charity Rogers (of Totnes).*
	6 January	*Elizabeth, daughter of Peter and Mary Clear.*
	20 January	*Arthur, son of Richard and Joan Smerdon.*
	24 February	*Mary, daughter/base child of Mary Nichols.*
	2 March	*John, son of Valentine and Hannah Hannaford.*
	24 March	*Richard Baker, son of Christopher and Agnes Niner.*
	18 June	*Richard, son of John and Grace Blight.*
	3 August	*Francis Garde, son of John and Frances Searle.*
	10 September	*William, son of Matthew and Mary Foall.*
	28 September	*Richard, son of Richard and Elizabeth Mugford.*
	27 October	*John, son of John and Mary Widdicombe.*
	19 December	*John Palfrey, son of John and Joanna Baker.*
	21 December	*Mary, daughter of Giles and Ann Shinner.*
	25 December	*Agnes, daughter of William and Mary Hannaford.*
1789	11 January	*John, son of Philip and Elizabeth Shapter.*
	14 January	*Mary, daughter of John Mitchell (Junr) and Joan Bidlake.*
	16 January	*Rebecca Shinner, daughter of Richard and Rebecca Trist.*
	25 January	*Wilmot, daughter of Andrew and Mary Watson.*
	8 March	*Susan, daughter of John and Susanna Petherbridge.*

	19 April	Thomas, son of John and Sarah Harris.
	6 May	Thomas Atwill, son of John and Sarah Watson.
	24 May	William, son of George (Junr) and Ann Penney.
	9 June	Robert Watson, son of John (Junr) and Mary Faremouth.
	5 July	William, son of William and Margaret Hollett.
	5 July	Nancy, daughter of John and Mary Godfree.
	19 July	William, son of Thomas and Elizabeth Rimes.
	29 July	John, son of Humphrey and Joan Watson.
1813	21 January	Harriet, daughter of Henry (Yeoman: Staple) and Elizabeth Searle.
	24 January	Mary, daughter of John (Carpenter) and Ann Gill.
	7 February	Thomas, son of William (Labourer) and Sarah Stentiford.
	20 March	Rebecca, daughter of Samuel (Labourer) and Agnes Barnes.
	16 April	Nicholas, son of John (Yeoman) and Elizabeth Shinner.
	6 June	Elizabeth, daughter of Henry (Labourer) and Elizabeth Pomroy.
	20 June	Derek, son of John and Elizabeth Phillips.
	7 November	James, son of William (Labourer) and Anne Hannaford.
	7 November	Sarah, daughter of Thomas (Labourer) and Elizabeth Osborn.
1814	5 January	John Niner, son of John (Yeoman) and Ann Watson.
	27 February	Thomas, son of James (Labourer) and Tammy Westaway.
	6 March	William Henry, son of William (Mariner) and Mary Huthings.
	19 May	Thomas, son of James (Labourer, Cobberton) and Grace Wyatt.
	19 June	Edmund, son of Iosiar (Shoemaker, Week) and Anne Whiteway.
	3 July	John, son of John (Mason, Week) and Agnes Nelder.
	16 July	George, son of Bartholemu (Labourer, Week) and Mary Putt.
	31 July	Susanna, daughter of Samuel (Labourer, Cobberton) and Ann Pack.
	31 July	Ann, daughter of William (Carpenter, Week) and Anne Parnell.
	17 September	Mary, daughter of Samuel (Labourer, Longcause) and Mary Stanlake.
	26 December	Henry, son/base child of Olive Whiteway.
1815	29 January	Thomas, son of Thomas (Labourer) and Grace Farley.
	12 February	Mary, daughter/base child of Elizabeth Miller.
	17 May	William, son of Henry (Yeoman, Staple) and Elizabeth Searle.
1816	7 January	Ann, daughter of Robert (Labourer, Totnes) and Mary Hannaford.
	21 January	Elizabeth, daughter of Thomas (Labourer) and Elizabeth Osborn.
	3 March	James, son of Thomas (Labourer) and Lolitia Morgan.
	28 April	William, son of William (Labourer) and Mary Webber.
	6 May	Margaret, daughter of George (Labourer) and Elizabeth Gidley.
	23 June	John, son of James (Labourer) and Grace Wyatt.
	7 July	William, son of Josias (Shoemaker) and Mary Ann Whiteway.
	6 October	Andrew, son of John (Farmer) and Mary Niner.
	29 December	Mary Ann, daughter of John (Labourer) and Mary Barnes.
1817	7 March	Elizabeth, daughter of William (Yeoman) and Anne Shinner.
	16 March	Ann, daughter of Samuel (Labourer) and Agnes Barnes.
	16 March	Mary Ann, daughter of Richard (Labourer) and Mary Hodge.
	23 March	Charles, son of James (Labourer) and Thamason Westerway.
	20 April	Ann, daughter of Humphry (Yeoman) and Harriet Watson.
	17 May	John Westerway, son/base child of Mary Allery.
	15 June	Ann, daugher of John (Yeoman) and Ann Watson.
	13 July	William, son of William (Butcher) and Mary Ann Luscombe.
	31 August	Joseph Alexanda, son of John (Carpenter) and Ann Gill.
	4 October	Joseph, son of John (Labourer) and Mary Barnes.
	16 November	Alicia, daughter of Thomas (Gardener) and Betsy Watson.
	17 November	Richard, son of Arthur and Louisa Champernowne.
	25 December	Richard, son of Henry (Labourer) and Elizabeth Searle.

1818	1 February	Richard, son of William (labourer) and Mary Webber.
	25 May	Louisa, daughter of John (Yeoman, Yarner) and Sarah Bidlake.
	23 August	Richard, son of Samuel (Mason) and Mary Parnell.
	10 October	Elizabeth, daughter of Peter (Carpenter) and Elizabeth Clear.

1819	11 April	Jane, daughter of Richard (Labourer) and Mary Hodge.
	23 May	Sarah, daughter of David (Mason) and Margaret Beer.
	30 May	Thomas and Robert, sons of John (Shoemaker) and Mary Beer.
	13 June	John son of John (Labourer) and Margaret Blackler.
	11 July	Anne Lolitia daughter of Thomas (Labourer) and Lolitia Morgan.
	5 September	Elizabethk daughter of John (Carpenter, Puddaven) and Anne Gill.
	7 November	John, son of John (Labourer, New Houses) and Mary Barnes.
	24 November	John, son of Thomas (Farmer, Cobberton) and Jane Clear.
	12 December	James Dundas, son of James (Mariner) and Anne Milnes (Cott).

1820	11 January	John, son of Arthur (Deceased) and Louisa Champernowne.
	5 March	Harriet, daughter of Humphry (Farmer, Barton) and Harriet Watson.
	19 March	Thomas Bartlett, son/base child of Anne Irish (Single: of Week).
	16 April	Mary Ann Wakeham, daugher/base child of Mary Luscombe (Single: of Forder).
	30 April	William, son of John (Mason, Cott) and Jane Parnell.
	14 May	Joseph, son of Samuel (Labourer, Woodicott) and Agnes Barnes.
	9 July	Fanny, daughter of John (Mason, Week) and Agnes Nelder.
	20 October	Lusanna, daughter of Henry (Labourer, Staple) and Elizabeth Searle.
	24 December	Mary, daughter of James (Labourer, Week) and Tamsine Westaway.

1821	20 January	Richard, son of John (Labourer) and Mary Blackler.
	11 February	Susan Hoskins, daughter of Peter (Blacksmith, Longcause) and Elizabeth Clear.
	25 February	Grace, daughter/base child of Roziah Lee.
	10 March	Mary, daughter of David (Mason, Week) and Margaret Beer.
	18 March	Jane, daughter of John (Labourer) and Mary Barnes.
	8 April	Henry, son of Humphrey (Farmer, Barton) and Harriet Watson.
	8 July	James, son/base child of Susann Hurford.
	15 July	William, son of John (Farmer, Billany) and Ann Watson.

1822	6 January	Henry, son of Thomas (Labourer, Staple) and Lolitia Morgan.
	20 January	Samuel, son of Samuel (Labourer, Longcause) and Mary Stanlake.
	10 March	John, son of John (Mason, Lownard) and Jane Parnell.
	7 July	Frances Langworthy, daughter of Giles (Labourer) and Frances Parnell.
	1 September	George Augustus, son of James (Gentleman, Cott) and Anne Milnes.
	10 November	William, son of George ('smith and Mariner) and Caroline Gill.
	24 November	Mary Ann, daughter/base child of Rebecca Barnes (Single).
	24 November	John, son of John (Blacksmith) and Elizabeth (Deceased) Shinner.

1823	5 January	Mary Ann, daughter of Peter (Blacksmith) and Elizabeth Clear.
	28 September	Hannah, daughter of Richard (Labourer) and Mary Hodge.
	25 December	Mary, daughter of John (Mason) and Jane Parnell.

1824	18 January	Susan, daughter of George (Labourer) and Elizabeth Gidley.
	14 March	Peter, son of Peter (Blacksmith) and Elizabeth Clear.
	27 June	Richard, second son/base child of Anne Irish (Single: of Week)

| 1825 | 25 November | Sarah, daughter of William (Labourer) and Susan Barnes. |
| | 25 December | Richard, son of John (Mason) and Jane Parnell. |

1826	5 February	Sarah, daughter of Richard (Labourer) and Mary Hodge.
	12 February	John, son of Thomas (Labourer: Week) and Mary Putt.
	14 February	William, son of Thomas (Labourer) and Martha Barnes.
	26 March	James, son of William (Labourer: Week) and Mary Harris.

	16 July	*George, son of John (Labourer: Staple) and Margaret Harris.*
	23 July	*Richard, son of Peter (Blacksmith, Longcause) and Elizabeth Clear.*
	17 September	*Henry, son of John (Labourer) and Susanne Wyatt.*
	24 September	*Marria, daughter of Henry (Labourer: Cott) and Elizabeth Jope.*
	1 October	*Thomas Hannaford, son of William (Labourer) and Mary Webber.*
	19 November	*Ann, daughter of Ian (Farmer: Cott) and Susan Stidston.*
	3 December	*John, son of John (Labourer: New Houses) and Rebecca Gribble.*
1827	7 January	*Richard, son of Nicholas (Thatcher: Forder) and Anne Braddon.*
	8 April	*Mary, daughter of Samuel (Labourer: Longcause) and Mary Stanlake.*
	29 April	*Jane, daughter of William (Labourer) and Jane Phillips.*
	1 July	*Jane, daughter of Joseph (Labourer) and Amews Brimecombe.*
	22 July	*Richard, son of John (Labourer) and Elizabeth Phillips.*
	5 August	*Jane, daughter of John (Mason) and Jane Parnell.*
	4 November	*Maria, daughter of David (Mason) and Margaret Barnes.*
	11 November	*Margaret, daughter of John (Labourer) and Margaret Blackler.*
	7 December	*Emma, daughter of Mathias (Farmer: Shinner's Bridge) and Jane Watson.*
1828	17 February	*John, son of John (Labourer) and Jane Miller.*
	17 February	*Sarah, daughter of Nicholas (Thatcher: Forder) and Anne Braddon.*
	21 February	*Walter, son of Humphrey (Yeoman: Dartington House) and Harriet Watson.*
	2 March	*Hannah Niner, daughter of John (Farmer: Billany) and Anne Watson.*
	10 March	*Alfred Danvers, son of John (Yeoman: Yarner) and Sarah Bidlake.*
	20 April	*Henry, son of William (Kiln burner) and Mary Whiteway.*
	27 April	*George Hoskins, son of Peter (Blacksmith) and Elizabeth Clear.*
	11 May	*Maria, daughter of William (Labourer: Lower Cott) and Susan Barnes.*
	11 May	*Joseph, son of Benjamin (Mason: Cott) and Elizabeth Turpin.*
	18 May	*Elizabeth, daughter of Thomas (Labourer) and Mary Putt.*
	29 June	*William Henry, son of Peter (Mason) and Sarah Nelder.*
	28 July	*Jane, daughter of Giles (Labourer) and Frances Parnell.*
	31 July	*James, son of John (Hood) and Jane Turner.*
	14 September	*Anne, daughter of William (Labourer) and Elizabeth Harris.*
	24 December	*Susan, daughter of John (Labourer) and Rebecca Gribble.*
1829	? March	*James, son of John (Mason) and Jane Parnell.*
	24 May	*William, son of William (Thatcher) and Anne Braddon.*
	6 September	*Catherine, daughter of Mathias (Farmer) and Jane Watson.*
	11 October	*Elizabeth, daughter of John (Labourer) and Elizabeth Phillips.*
	1 November	*Ann, daughter of William (Labourer) and Jane Phillips.*
1830	7 March	*Caroline, daughter of Humphrey (Yeoman) and Harriet Watson.*
	20 June	*George, son of William (Labourer) and Susan Barnes.*
	11 July	*William, son of John (Labourer) and Mary Blackler.*
	19 September	*Thirza, daughter of Thomas (Labourer) and Mary Putt.*
1831	23 January	*Henry, son of David (Mason) and Margaret Beer.*
	23 January	*Anne, daughter of John (Mason) and Jane Parnell.*
	4 August	*William, son of William (Thatcher) and Mary Ann Braddon.*
	23 October	*James, son of John (Labourer: New Houses) and Elizabeth Phillips.*
	4 December	*James, son/base child of Susan Barret (Single: Lower Cott).*
1832	26 March	*William, son of Peter (Blacksmith) and Elizabeth Clear.*
	4 April	*George, son of John (Mason) and Jane Parnell.*
	10 June	*Henry, son/base child of Agnes Nelder (Single).*
	24 June	*Mary Henning, daughter of John (Carpenter: Longcause) and Margaret Clear.*
	12 August	*Charles, son of William (Labourer) and Susanna Barret.*
	11 September	*Thomas Harris, son of Humphrey (Yeoman: Dartington House) and Harriet Watson.*
	5 November	*Benjamin, son of Benjamin (Mason: Cott) and Elizabeth Turpin.*

1833	5 May	Henry, son of William (Labourer) and Elizabeth Harris.
	7 May	Mathias, son of Mathias (Farmer: Shinner's Bridge) and Jane Watson.
	16 June	Henry, son of John (Labourer) and Elizabeth Phillips.
	22 September	Margaret Ann, daughter of John (Labourer) and Margaret Blackler.
	21 October	Caroline, daughter of Mary Ann Luscombe (Widow).
	17 November	Susan, daughter of William (Labourer) and Jane Phillips.
	3 December	Charles Frederick, son of Humphrey (Lt Col, Hood Manor) and Jane Hill.

1834	16 February	John Baker, son of John (Carpenter) and Margaret Cleer.
	13 April	Susan, daughter of Nicholas (Thatcher) and Anne Braddon.
	8 June	Crispin Prideaue, son of William (Labourer: Cobberton) and Catharine Putt.
	21 June	Alice Jane, daughter of Henry Hocking (Blacksmith) and Maria Clear.
	9 August	Richard Henning, son of John (Carpenter) and Margaret Clear.
	7 September	Susan, daughter of John (Labourer) and Jane Miller.
	8 September	Sarah Harris, daughter of Humphrey (Yeoman) and Harriet Watson.
	24 September	Richard, son of Humphrey (Lt Col, Hood Manor) and Jane Hill.
	16 December	Frederick, son of Mathias (Yeoman) and Jane Watson.

1835	4 January	George, son of John (Labourer) and Elizabeth Phillips.
	8 February	Reuben, son of Benjamin (Mason: Cott) and Elizabeth Turpin.
	1 March	John, son of John (Shoemaker: Week) and Dinah Beer.
	5 July	Makalah, daughter of Thomas (Labourer) and Mary Putt.
	9 August	Richard, son of John (Labourer) and Rebecca Gribble.
	23 August	Henry, joint son/base child of Margaret Gidley (Single: Cobberton).
	24 August	Elizabeth Caroline, daughter of John (Gentleman: Dartington House) and Jane Hill.
	1 November	Frederick, son of William (Labourer) and Susanna Barret.
	15 November	Samuel, son of John (Mason) and Jane Parnell.

1836	17 January	Mary, daughter of Edward (Farmer) and Alice Parnell.
	14 February	Samuel Henry, son of Samuel (Labourer) and Ellen Barnes.
	12 June	Edwin, son of John (Shoemaker: Week) and Dinah Beer.
	17 June	James, son of William (House servant: Dartington and Denbury) and Elizabeth Westaway.
	31 July	Elizabeth, daughter of William (Labourer) and Jane Phillips.
	14 August	Mary Anne, daughter of William and Mary Braddon. (Stated to have been privately baptised at Totnes in 1829.)
	14 August	Emma, daughter of William and Mary Anne Braddon. (Stated to have been privately baptised in 1833.)
	14 August	George Henry, son of William and Mary Anne Braddon.
	18 December	Nicholas, son of Nicholas (Thatcher) and Anne Braddon.

1837	5 February	William Thomas, son of Thomas (Pvt soldier: Dartington) and Grace Ford.
	26 February	Elizabeth, daughter of John (Labourer) and Elizabeth Phillips.
	23 April	Jane, daughter of Benjamin (Mason) and Elizabeth Turpin.
	7 May	George, son of Henry (Blacksmith: Venlow Cottage) and Mary Clear.
	19 November	Sarah, daughter of Samuel (Labourer) and Ellen Barnes.
	25 December	Emma, daughter of John (Shoemaker) and Dinah Beer.

1838	21 January	Margaret, daughter of John (Carpenter) and Margaret Clear.
	24 March	Sarah, daughter of Richard (Labourer) and Jane Winchester.
	1 April	Elizabeth, daughter of James (Servant) and Christian Putt.
	4 August	?, son of John (Labourer) and Elizabeth Phillips.
	16 September	John Collins, son of John (Labourer) and Elizabeth Anne Brimecombe.
	21 October	Samuel, son of Richard (Thatcher) and Elizabeth Williams.
	12 November	Lucy Wood, daughter/base child of Elizabeth Pack (Single). (Privately baptised.)

| 1839 | 13 January | Maria, daughter/base child of Maria Page (Widow). (Said to have been born on 13 May 1836). |

	1 February	*William James, son of John (Labourer) and Elizabeth Westaway.*
	25 March	*John, son of Samuel (Labourer) and Ellen Barnes.*
	18 April	*Arthur, son of Henry and Charlotte Champernowne.*
	5 May	*Thomas, son of Thomas (Labourer) and Mary Putt.*
	18 August	*Owen Henry, son of Henry (Blacksmith) and Maria Clear.*
	19 September	*Jane, daughter of Matthew (Carpenter: Staverton Bridge) and Jane Hill.*
	13 October	*Mary, daughter of James (Footman: Shinner's Bridge) and Jane Westaway.*
1840	*14 June*	*William, son of William (Footman) and Elizabeth Westaway.*
	24 June	*Henry, son of Henry and Charlotte Champernowne.*
	28 June	*Jane, daughter of Nicholas (Thatcher) and Anne Braddon.*

Longcause Barracks, Barracks Hill

When the Napoleonic Wars broke out in 1793, and British Government thought there might be the risk of an invasion of French forces from across the Channel, barracks were built at Longcause (Barracks Hill) in 1794 to garrison Totnes and the surrounding area and to guard routes to Plymouth and Buckfastleigh. Various regiments occupied the barracks during the war years, some for about a year, others for much longer. The Worcester Militia were the first to move in during 1794. The various regiments to occupy the barracks for the duration of the Wars, from 1793 to 1815, were:

1794	Worcester Militia
1795	North Devon Hussars
1796–99	Berkshire Regiment
1798	Surrey Light Dragoons
1798–1800	Cornish Militia
1799	East Devon Regiment
1805	4th Dragoon Guards
1807	3rd Dragoon Guards
1810–11	9th Light Dragoons
1814	26th Regiment of Foot

In 1815, with the defeat of Napoleon, the barracks were no longer required and were later sold to John Brown of Ashburton, who built Longcause House in 1823 on the site of the former officers' mess, keeping the original cellars, which still exist today. In 1892 P.H. Champernowne gave the house to a Miss Caroline Martin who, in her will, bequeathed it to William A. Martin. He died in 1949. The property was purchased by George Reeves, who lived there until 1976. The present owner is Keith Sykes.

Longcause House, built in 1825.

Church House, Week, in 2003. The first village school (1800–1844), in 1911 it became a working men's club.

Dartington Primary School, built at Shinner's Bridge in 1855, pictured in July 2005.

✦ CHAPTER 3 ✦

Schools and Education

State education was not compulsory until 1870, but for parents who wanted their children to read and write, some provisions existed for which the parish paid. There are occasional references in the Poor Rate records with such entries as: 'April 1800: paid for schooling Anne Hannaford £1.4s.0d'; 'Rulland and Rimes schooling (*two parishioners*) 2s.0d.'

The services of 'instructors' were fairly cheap and they were often used to teach practical skills, as cloth was still being woven on domestic looms in around 1800: 'Paid by Anne Dingel for instructing Mary Searle to weave 12s.6d.'.

In 1800 the old Church House was repaired and converted into a village school with money which had accumulated from a long unclaimed annual rent from the yarn market at Ashburton, originally a legacy for supplying the poor people of Dartington with religious books. The Revd R.H. Froude, rector of the parish and well-known historian, was responsible for the annuity being used in this way.

An entry states:

John Ford, by his will dated 8 March 1667, gave out of his Tuesday's market at Ashburton, for selling wool and

yarn, unto the rector and churchwardens of the parish of Dartington, and their successors, an annuity of 40s., to be by them bestowed in English Bibles, and, on every New-year's-day, distributed to the poor people and children of the said parish, as they should think fit.

This annuity is under the same circumstances as that of £8 given by the same donor, out of the same market, for the benefit of the poor of Ashburton, as mentioned in the present report in account of the charities of that place. In consequence of the cessation of the Tuesday's wool and yarn market, nothing is now received by the parish of Dartington. In 1800, the rector received from the then owner of this market the arrears of this gift for 20 years to that time, which were applied towards fitting up a schoolhouse in the parish, and in the purchase of books. No payment has been since made in respect of this annuity.

When the Charity Commissioners reported on the parish charities in 1822, they referred to the school as being held in a part of the Church House, and noted that considerable money had been spent since 1802

The Gothic-style window at the east end of the primary school.

The drinking fountain (1902) at the entrance to Shinner's Bridge Primary School, Summer 2005.

Shinner's Bridge Primary School, 1903. The children identified include, left to right, back row: *Louis Miller, Cyril Parnell, Percy Barnes, Henry Almond, Frank Crook, Arthur Stanning, Frank Lock, Arthur Edmonds, Edwin Hodge, Phillip Barker, George Casely, William Hodge, Lorna Dennis, Louie Edmonds, Florence Kearley, Elsie Kearley, Edith Casely, Louie Arscott, Gertrude Hames;* girls, second row: *Winifred Kearley, Louie Barnes, Gladys Hodge, Maud Tucker, Emily Tucker, Jane Lucas, Bessie Clear, Winifred Almond, Lena Crook.*

Dartington School group, early 1920s. Left to right, back row: *Wilfred Holwell, Stanley Tucker, Frank Tucker, Sidney Cook, ? Rowe, Bim Edmonds;* third row: *Tom Hodge, Grace Pedrock, Dorothy Farley, Ivy Edmonds, May Barnes, Vera Western, Gwen Cater, Clarence Miller;* second row: *Alice Hawkins, Loveda Howell, Ruth Holwell, Beatrice Tucker, Kathleen Tucker, Lil Miller;* front row: *Jack Kinsman, Gerald Luscombe, Donald Price, Walter Barker.*

Dartington School children, mid-1920s. Left to right, back row: *?, Phyllis Passmore, ?, Elsie Hext, Edgar Holwell, ?;* middle row: *Robert Veale, Ernest Cater, John Shinner, ?;* front row: *Amy Harvey, Christine Western, Mary Hodge, Teeny Cater, Lucia Jones, William Jones, William Barnes, John Sercombe.*

Lottie Mathews in the 1940s. She taught at the village school for many years.

on converting it for this purpose. Payment is mentioned of a salary of £5.5s. a year to a school-master until 1812. The Feoffees' accounts of the period record this annual payment to a schoolmaster called Coombe, the first payment being in 1803. This being also the date of the first reference to the School House, this might be when the first Parish School was established.

The Church House was not close to the church at Dartington Hall, where you would expect, but at Week, a hamlet $1\frac{1}{2}$ miles distant. The reason for this location is unknown – it certainly did not fulfil one of the main functions of a Church House, which was to serve the convenience of parishioners attending church from the far corners of the scattered parish. It is known, however, that other facilities were provided near the church, in a building described in the Feoffees' and churchwardens' accounts as the Church Stables, which were equipped with 'privies'. Leonard Elmhirst identified the Church Stables as the west end of the building, later known as Barton Workshop, largely rebuilt in later years.

That the Church House was at Week, as local tradition affirms, is evident from references, albeit oblique, in the Feoffees' accounts. The various descriptions used – Week House, Church House and School House – are all, as is clear from the cross refer-

Primary schoolchildren in the 1950s. The photograph includes: Linda Holwell, Sheena Powsland, Ann Stevens, Hazel Lock, Ann Jones, Beryl Boon, Susan Whitehead, Nicola Cornish, Delia Taylor, Coral Freeston, Roger Bunce, Michael Edwards, Michael O'Donague, Richard Fulcher and John Miles.

Dartington Primary School, 1951. Left to right, back row: Shirley Harris, Suzette Browning, Shirley Clements, Betty James, Dorothy Cole, Carol Taylor; third row: Jane Langer, Prudence Coaker, Jennifer Barnes, Heather Freestone, Ann Lock, Ann Hill, Margaret Passmore, Pat Barkwell, Gwen Denham; second row: John Rowse, Jimmy Crook, Peter Watkins, John Wilson, Barry Nash, Mr John Heaps, Victor Gould, Edward Endicott, Graham Knowles, Alan Clake, Gordon MacLening; front row: Terry Kerswell, John Hillson, Brian Lake, Derek Edgell, Michael Langer, William O'Flarathy, David Parsons, Melvyn Prowse, Mervyn Batten.

Schoolchildren at Totnes Station, c.1950, setting off on a school trip to Oxford. The group includes John Heaps (headmaster), Miss Nichols (teacher), Basil Clake, Bill Parnell, Heather White, Diana Knowles, Rosemary Kerswell, Joy Edwards, Alan Brown, Marilyn Edgell, Mervyn Batten, Alan Clake, David Parsons, Gwen Denham, Susan Ingham, Derek Jewell, Peter James, Clifford Jewell, Doreen Codd, Janet Langdon, Vivien Gardener, Anthony Parnell, Gwen Edwards, Irene Clements, Valerie Hard, Pat Knowles, Clare Bunce, John Wilson, Peter Watkins, Mrs White, Mrs Batten, Mr and Mrs Kerswell, Mrs Parsons, Mrs Parnell, Mrs Miller, Mrs Rogers, Mrs Codd, Mrs Hard, Mrs Denham, Mrs Knowles, Mrs Ingham and Ida Barnes.

Junior class, c.1950. Left to right, back row: Ruth Barkwell, Sandra Taylor, Pat Lock, Cynthia Jones, Clare Bunce, Doreen Codd, Miss Nichols; third row: Diane Wickham, Ann Dray, Judith Langer, Pauline Miller, Pat Price, Joy Edwards, Diane Knowles, Elizabeth Hard, Annitje Last; kneeling: Peter James, Geoffrey Wood, Andrew MacLening, Clifford Jewell, Terry Rogers, Alan Brown, Alan Tucker; sitting: Derek Boon, Peter Codd, Stuart Giles, Fernley Harris, Ian Redshaw, Peter Clake, Mervyn Langdon, John Coaker.

The school football team, 1955/56. Left to right, back row: *Geoffrey Wood, Clifford Jewell, Bobby Widger, Tony Brown, Bill Parnell, David Mann;* front row: *Peter MacTaggart, Terry Rogers, Derek Boon, Peter James, Peter Codd, John Coker, Peter Clake.*

Infant class, May 1974. Left to right, back row: *Margaret Wood (Infant assistant), Susan Bamforth, Marian Wellum, Ann Terry, Joanne Ramsden, Zoe Lovell, Robert Zeally, Mrs Range (teacher);* middle row: *David Stone, Alison Miller, Jonathan Gillson, Lisa Osborne, Patrick Evans, Christian Iversen, Timothy Michelmore, Rachael Kelly, Rebecca Norman, Gareth George;* front row: *Catherine Hyack, Andrew Miller, Sophie Dix, James Wallbank, Sheila Giles, Sarah Hopkins, Justin Miles, Helen Prout, Philip Hatch, Guy Rogers.*

Primary School infants. c.1978.

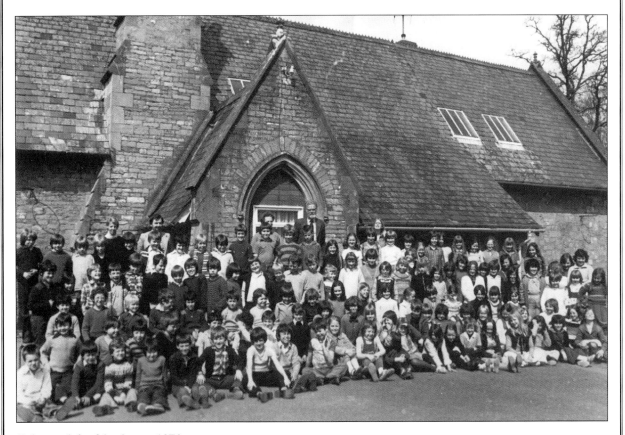

Primary School juniors. c.1978.

Dartington men Phillip Sercombe, John Gallon and Tony Covachich, who all served in the 1982 Falklands War, with Primary schoolchildren.

ences, of the same premises. Tenancies granted of parts of Week House are later confirmed by rent payments from the same tenants for what is then called the School House; the letting of rooms at 'the school house' to Rebecca Barrett is associated with a record of a receipt of the appropriate rent payment for 'a room at the Church House', and there is more than one reference to 'the School House at Week'. The poorhouse was also at Week, but whether or not it was part of the Church House is not certain. It is clear that at some time in the early-nineteenth century parts of the Church House were occupied by poor persons, and a reference in the Feoffees' accounts of 1837 refers to 'the old and infirm who may be living in the Poorhouse and Church House'.

The Feoffees' accounts reveal that the school was conducted on the ground floor of the Church House and may have consisted of two rooms, e.g.: In 1833 there was a resolution 'that a new lime-ash floor be laid in the small room of the Schoolhouse at Week'; an entry in 1842 reads: 'Rent from Thomas Beer for a room over the schoolrooms'; and in 1844 'Whitewashing two rooms at Schoolhouse'.

The Tithe Apportionment Schedule of 1839 gives Tithe No. 272a as a house occupied by 'Ann Parnell and others'. This seems a particularly inadequate description of the Church House/School House,

even though the part of the building occupied by the school might be exempt from tithes. What is significant, however, in the identification of the building, is that in the Feoffees' accounts from 1839 to 1852 the payment of Poor Rates and Way Rates on the Church House are recorded in respect of its occupation by what are evidently poor persons and described as 'Ann Parnell and others', as in the Tithe Apportionment Schedule.

The Church House, which accommodated the first parish school, is identified as Tithe No. 272 and, at the time of writing, the first house on the right entering Week from the direction of the church and standing back from the road is known as Church House Cottage.

The references to the schoolhouse continue throughout the remainder of the Feoffees' accounts up to 1852, when the accounts ceased, and it is assumed that the school continued in the Church House until the new school was built in 1855. Considerable structural alterations were made to the Church House during 1859, involving the building of a partition wall, new chimneys and windows, all of which suggest, perhaps, the vertical division of the building into separate cottages.

The new school at Shinner's Bridge was built in 1855 by the Revd R. Champernowne on a site given by Mr A. Champernowne of Dartington Hall and consisted of one schoolroom. It was built in heavy Gothic style and with a large, pointed arched window at the east end. The schoolroom was also intended to serve for divine worship and was licensed by the Bishop on 1 June 1878 so that it could be used between the demolition of the old church at the hall and the completion of the new one in 1880.

In 1884 the schoolroom was extended in length and an infants' classroom built on the north side. Mr. P.G. David was headmaster for 40 years (1868–1908).

A drinking fountain was installed in the boundary wall in 1902 to commemorate the coronation of King Edward VII and Queen Alexandra.

Though the premises were privately provided, the school became a National School and continued as such until after the 1902 Act, when the LEA assumed responsibility for its maintenance as a Voluntary Church School. It is still a Voluntary School, having assumed Controlled status in 1951 under the provisions of the 1944 Act.

In 1939 the senior (age 11) children were transferred to the newly built Senior School, at Ashburton Road on the outskirts of Totnes, which in 1948 became Redworth and in 1966 King Edward VI Community College.

To accommodate the rising number of children in the parish, the county authority leased an adjoining site in 1954 (part of the cider mill, which closed in 1952) and acquired the cider pound and Dutch barn which stood on it, to convert into a hall and other school facilities.

Other Schools

According to County Directories, an Infants school was started at Week between 1866 and 1870, and closed sometime between 1883 and 1889. Its closure probably coincided with the opening of the new infants' classroom at the National School in 1884.

Directories also record a girls' school at Brooking in 1873, supported by the Champernowne family, which was closed in 1900. No reference can be found to the building.

Foxhole School

Designed by Oswald P. Milne and built in 1931/32, Foxhole was first used as a Junior School then as a Senior School for Dartington Hall School. The children of many of the day's celebrities were pupils at the school, the majority of them being boarders, some of them from overseas. There was an outdoor swimming pool where nude bathing was allowed, which caused controversy with outsiders from time to time. In the late 1940s and early 1950s the pool was often used discreetly by village teenagers when the school was closed for summer holidays!

The number of pupils gradually declined and the school finally closed in 1987. The building is now used as offices and accommodation for Dartington College of Arts students, while the site of the pool has become part of a car park.

Brimhay Nursery School

Brimhay Nursery School was built in 1970 at a cost of

Foxhole School.

Brimhay Nursery School golden jubilee celebrations, 2002. L–r: *Jamie and Alexander Williams, Kieran Holland.*

£20,000, Edna Pitman being its first headmistress. The school is built on three levels, the ground floor being the general play area, with washrooms for quick access from the play areas. The middle floor was an open area for music, dancing and singing, while an adjacent kitchen was used for cooking school meals on the premises. The top floor, light and airy, was used for arts and crafts, with an area for quiet reading. Outside is an area for riding tricycles and scooters, etc., and a grass area to play on. A small swimming pool, in use for many years, encourages the early development of swimming skills.

Brimhay Nursery School.

CHAPTER 4

Dartington's Churches

The Church of St Mary the Virgin

On Friday, 8 May 1878, work started on the dismantling of the medieval church at Dartington Hall, where the earliest record of a rector dates back to 1226.

Two months later, on Saturday, 10 July, the foundation stone of a new church was laid in a more central position, on glebe land near the parsonage (now the Old Postern) and closer to Week, the main centre of population. While the church was being built, services were held in the school at Shinner's Bridge. The new church was consecrated on 27 April 1880 by Frederick Temple, Bishop of Exeter and, subsequently, Archbishop of Canterbury, and the first service was held on Sunday, 2 May 1880. The cost, £5,3101.4s.4d., was largely met by the rector, Richard Champernowne, with some assistance from his nephew, Arthur Champernowne, squire and patron of the living. Architect John Loughborough Pearson was already engaged in designing Truro Cathedral, and at Dartington he stuck to the exact ground plan of the old church, even rebuilding the turrets with

stairs to the rood-loft, when only the central part of the rood-screen remained.

The roofs follow the same plan as in the old church. The Beer stone arcades from the old church were re-erected on Portland stone bases to make them loftier. The mouldings of the chancel windows were used again, and the windows in the nave aisles were brought into harmony with the chancel windows. Limestone from the Shinner's Bridge quarry was used for the outside walls, while the dressings were of the Box Ground type of stone.

The tower is completely new work, its rich decorations being the work of Harry Hems. Each side of the tower carries, high up, the carved figure of one of the Evangelists. The battlements along the north and south aisles are medieval, while those around the chancel are additions of Pearson's. In the outer east wall of the chancel can be seen the foundation stone. High up in the eastern gable is the statue of the Virgin, St Mary, and the Child, and the gable is crowned with a foliated cross. These, once again, are works by Harry Hems.

The porch has a fine star-vault of fifteenth-century

St Mary's Church, Dartington, March 2006.

The porch and main door, with sanctuary knocker.

The medieval font, the oldest part of the church. Note the clasp, which would once have secured a cover.

workmanship, which comes from the old church. The angels at the corners have mostly been recarved, and the central boss in the roof is much worn. It has often been said to depict the White Hart of Richard II, a device used by the Holand family. One authority held that it represented the head of our Lord. Each year swallows nest in the vaulting of the porch roof. The main door is of great antiquity, with what appears to be a sanctuary knocker.

The oldest part of the church is the font, its octagonal bowl of rough moorstone granite dating far into the Middle Ages. Here parishioners have been baptised for many generations. The pedestal on which it stands is later, and the clasp in the side of the font dates from times when the font cover was locked to prevent thefts of holy water.

The pulpit, made at the end of the fifteenth century – the accounts for 1499 imply it was under

The church nave, 1997.

The high altar, which was originally in the old Dartington Hall Church.

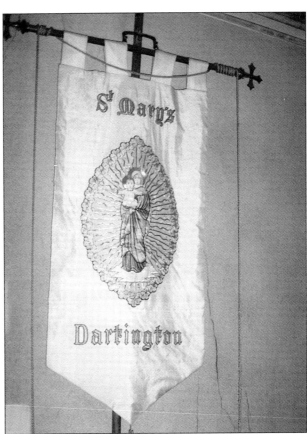

St Mary's Church standard.

Plaque in memory of Arthur Melville Champernowne.

construction at that time – was carefully restored in memory of a former rector, Charles Martin. Originally, statues of saints would have stood in the niches. Here preached the Tractarian friends of Richard Hurrell Froude, the archdeacon's eldest son, including John Keble and J.H. Newman, who was later to become cardinal. The latter's sermon at Dartington on 21 July 1831, with the title 'Scripture, a Record of Human Sorrow', was published afterwards.

The screen is much restored. Fifteenth-century work survives in the sections across the nave, but the groining and the sections across the side-aisles are careful work by Read's of Exeter. The screen was completed in 1913 as a memorial to John Plumer of Allerton by his relations.

There is in Denbury Parish Church a screen in the north transept which was removed from Dartington in the mid-nineteenth century. It would have been a parclose screen between the chancel and one of the side-chapels in the old church.

The screen at the west end of the nave was put up by the Stone family in 1912. The reredos provides a simple foil to the elaborate screen, paid for by public subscription in 1906.

The high altar, brought from the old church, was installed in 1836 by Archdeacon Froude, in fulfilment of a project started by his son, Hurrell Froude, who

had died earlier that year. The design is based on that of the high altar at Cologne Cathedral, and copies of the Dartington altar are to be found in several churches in this county. It was made from oak from the roof of the great hall at Dartington Hall, which had just been taken down. Without its marble base, the altar was very low, made so to suit the Archdeacon, who was short. In effect, the high altar is Hurrell Froude's memorial. The marble base was replaced by a new wooden one when the altar was moved out from the east wall in 1994.

The organ was built by Mr Speechley of London in about 1865 and stood in the parsonage for some years before the new church was ready for it. The pews and the choir stalls were made for the old church during Pearson's restoration. When they

St Mary's church choir in the late 1940s. Left to right, back row: Jean King, Violet Dommett, Rendle Crang, Cecil Cope, Jack Farley, Herbert Jeffery, Harold Cole, Barbara King; front row: Arthur Williams, John Laskey, Terry Parsons, Mrs Last (organist), William Hext, Revd Edwards, Sidney Harris, Mr Richards (churchwarden), David Cole, John Eddy.

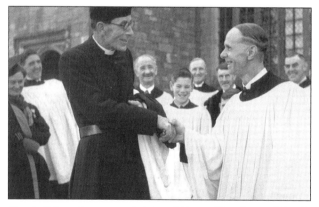

Revd Edwards congratulates Sidney Harris on his 50 years in the Dartington church choir, from 1898 to 1948.

were moved to the new church they fitted, the building being the same size.

The south chapel was rebuilt as the Champernowne family pew. In the east wall of this chapel two medieval carved stone brackets have been inserted, presumably designed to carry the statues of saints (a medieval piscine with carved foliage is to be found in the vestry). In 1953 the pew was converted into a chapel and furnished as part of the war memorial. An aumbry, given in memory of Mrs Maisie Scales, was dedicated in 1975. Here the sacrament can be reserved: very appropriately, the crucifixion in the window above making this corner of the church very suitable for a Jesus chapel.

The east and south chancel windows, and the east window of the Jesus chapel, retain their medieval tracery. Note the star in the tracery in the side-chapel, a feature largely confined to certain churches in this district. The glass is good Victorian work by Messrs Clayton & Bell. The east chancel window depicts the Christ as Pentocrator, almighty Ruler, surrounded by the heavenly circle of saints and angels.

The fine peal of six bells was cast from the peal of five bells removed from the old tower in 1878. Some of these bells were medieval, one bearing the inscription, *'Protégé Virgo pia, quos convoco sancta Maria'*. The early churchwardens' accounts record payment for a new bell from funds raised in the main from 'tavernings of ale'. The bells were rehung in 1932.

The church plate (kept for safety in the bank) includes an Elizabethan chalice, late-seventeenth-century flagons, a chalice and a tazza. The parish registers, now deposited at the County Record Office, go back to 1538.

The kneelers were embroidered by the Ladies' Guild of Helpers, led by Mrs Sally Morris. Among their other works were vestments and a portable lectern.

The Parish Church of St Mary, Dartington, is a handsome structure and a fine example of church building of its period. Pearson, one of the leading architects of his day, at Dartington very skilfully and unobtrusively adapted the main features of a medieval church to meet the needs of later generations.

Unlike most towns and villages, Dartington has no war memorial, but on either side of the church walls, a roll of honour names those men of the parish who gave their lives in the two world wars. The Church of St Barnabas at Brooking has a war memorial for the First World War only.

Rectors of Dartington

1152	Michael
1226	Theobald Sancto Jovians
1261	Henry de Sicca Villa
1307	Thomas Ulcio
1314	Sir Thomas de Bradforde
1318	Sir Simon de Raleghe
1349	Thomas Barnhouse
1373	Peter Hartebrigge
1411	Peter Overton
27 Jan 1414	Ralph Walwayn
7 July 1418	John Bowen
30 Apr 1453	John Germayn, died 1460
1467	William Havery
7 July 1468	Richard Goodfellow
2 Nov 1500	Robert Welby
15 Jun 1501	John Stephan, died 1560
1565	Thomas Clavicye
12 Jun 1569	Miles Leigh
27 Jun 1577	William Parre
18 Feb 1586	Griffen Jones, died 1593
12 Nov 1593	Robert Bruxham
8 Feb 1596	Edward Costerd
12 Apr 1636	Thomas Loveys
2 Jan 1661	Henry Skynner
26 Mar 1669	John Ford
8 Jan 1679	Nicholas Rooke
23 Sep 1731	John Acland, resigned
27 Jan 1737	Francis Champernowne
17 Aug 1763	James Andrew
27 Oct 1764	Francis Yarde
12 Apr 1799	Robert Hurrell Froude
1859	Richard Champernowne
1891	Charles Martin, died
1910	Walter Eustace Cox, retired
1921	John Sturges Martin
27 Jan 1940	Roland Alexander Edwards
1948	Cannon of Norwich
23 Oct 1948	Leslie Gilbert Ketchley, retired 1956
2 Oct 1956	Quintin Morris, retired 1970
23 Nov 1971	John Graham Bishop, also Vicar of Rattery, 1979
8 Apr 1992	Paul Wimsett
30 July 1999	Neil Gair Batcock, May 2006 to Norfolk
20 March 2007	Joanna Abecassis also Vicar of Brooking

St Barnabas Church, Brooking.

The Church of St Barnabas, Brooking

Built in 1855 by the Revd Richard Champernowne, the Church of St Barnabas is situated close to the Plymouth road (Tigley) near the hamlet of Brooking, approximately two miles west of the main village, on the fringe of the parish. Designed by the architect G.F. Pearson, its marble pillars are reputed to have been carved from stone from 'Pit Parks' quarry near

St Barnabas Church altar and stained-glass window.

Beryl Gill, organist at St Barnabas for over 28 years.

The font, St Barnabas.

the Old Parsonage at Dartington. The full-length spire is unique, most churches in Devon having a tower. The organ, recently overhauled, is one of only two of its type in the country; Beryl Gill was the organist for over 28 years. The Casely family had strong links with the church – George Casely was sexton for 30 years – and Miss M. Casely tolled the bell during the First World War. The Kellock family from Allerton also had an interest for many years.

Harvest Thanksgiving Services at Brooking, Dartington

A harvest thanksgiving service was held in the Church of St Barnabas, Brooking, on Sunday last. The sacred edifice was profusely decorated with flowers, fruit and corn, special care being bestowed on the altar and font. On the superaltar were four vases of choice flowers, two candle-sticks, with three lights in each and two minia-ture sheaves of wheat. On the font was placed a beau-tiful floral cross and at its base different kinds of fruit embedded in moss. The Service, which was a full choral evensong, commenced by the surpliced choir singing the hymn, 'Come ye thankful people, come', as a proces-sional. The special psalms chosen for the occasions were those for the 12th day of the month, sung to Anglican chants. Tallis' renowned festival responses were used and were very fairly rendered by the choir. The other hymns were Nos 224, 300 and 130 (Hymns Ancient and Modern), the latter being most heartily given both by the choir and congregation. The Revd R. Champernowne intoned the service and the Revd W.W. Goodacre, the incumbent of Brooking, preached an appropriate and thoroughly practical sermon. The congregation was very large, numbers being unable to find seats. The offertory (which was in aid of the Indian Famine Relief Fund), having been collected and the blessing given, the choir proceeded down the Church, singing, 'Onward Christian Soldiers'. Thus was brought to a close one of the most hearty services ever heard within St Barnabas Church.

From the Totnes Times
6 October 1877

The war memorial at St Barnabas to those who died in the First World War.

Dartington Marriages and Christenings

The wedding of Mr Turner and Miss Gill, 1912.

The wedding of Frederick Widger and Gladys Hodge, 1922.

The wedding of Reginald Newson and Violet Young,
16 November 1932.

The wedding of Victor Parnell and Ivy Edmonds,
17 April 1933.

The wedding of Hezekiah Morgan and Dorothy Miller, August 1933.

The wedding of Tommy Nash and Prudence Mary Hodge, late 1940s.

The wedding of Peter Sutcliffe and Joan Widger, 22 June 1946

The wedding of Derek Lake and Dorothy Denham, c.1950

The wedding of Edgar Hodge and Beryl Gill, 27 August 1949.

The wedding of John Sercombe and Elsie Mann, October 1950.

The wedding of Peter Hodge and Margaret James, 2 August 1954.

Left: *The wedding of*
Stanley Quaintance and
Cynthia Taylor,
3 September 1955.

The wedding of Jack James and Margaret Hollyer,
29 March 1958.

The wedding of Tony Beard and Wendy Selleck, 24 October 1959.

The wedding of Brian Piller and Rosemary Tuffnell, 26 March 1960.

The christening of Steven John Hodge, October 1957

The christening of Steven Paul Roberts, September 1964.

The christening of Jamie Williams by Revd Neil Batcock, 16 August 1999.

The christening of Jamie and Alexander Williams, with parents Chris and Lisa, August 1999.

Alexander and grandad Colin Osborne, August 1999.

William 'Bill' Passmore, 5th Devons, and his sisters, Gladys and Audrey.

Hans Blix and Booms Adaisy

Have we really had the proof,
Are they telling us the truth?
Must we start another war
and give the world more blood and gore?
Politicians dream up these wars
and lead our youth through the devil's doors.
All on this planet are of humankind,
but how many human beings will we find?
And when this saving of the world is done
Will we know who really won?

William G. MacLening
Resident

CHAPTER 5

The War Years

The First World War

On 26 June 1914 in Sarajevo, the Archduke Franz Ferdinand, the first heir apparent to the throne of Austria-Hungary, and his wife, Sophie, were assassinated by Gavrilo Prinzip, a Bosnian anarchist.

Austria-Hungary made such heavy demands for compensation that Serbia refused to comply. On 28 July, Austria-Hungary, supported by Germany, declared war; Russia and France backed Serbia. On 1 August Germany declared war on Russia and France and marched into Luxembourg. The following day The German Army invaded neutral Belgium,

Card sent from a soldier in France to his young daughter.

The British War Medal (left) *and the Victory Medal, awarded during the First World War.*

ignoring Britain's ultimatum; at 11p.m. on 4 August Britain declared war on Germany: The 'Great War' had begun. On 8 August, the first troops of the British Expeditionary Force crossed the Channel, disembarking at French ports to fight alongside Britain's ally.

On 18 September 1914, F. Revell, clerk to the Parish Council and assistant overseer, asked to be relieved of his duties so that he could enlist. He returned in November 1919, after more than five years of military service. A 'recruiting march' which took place in the parish in April 1915 was not very successful.

On 5 January 1916 the Conscription Bill was introduced, followed, on 10 February, by the introduction of compulsory military service for single men aged 19-30 and on 2 March by the Military Service Act.

On 16 April 1917, Mr J.S. Smerdon, Chairman of the Parish Council, stated that, 'Up to the present, very few men from the Parish have enrolled under the government's National Service Act.'

From 12 May 1917 men between 41 and 50 were accepted for the Army.

On 11 November 1918 at 11.00a.m. hostilities ceased and there was an armistice with Germany, and on 28 June 1919 Germany signed a peace treaty and the League of Nations was formed.

Peace celebrations took place in the parish, with a church service, sports, a public tea and dancing in the Shinner's Bridge school playground.

Princess Mary's Gift Box

Princess Mary (later the Princess Royal) organised a fund to ensure that each man serving in France at

Princess Mary's 1914 Christmas Gift Box.

Dartington Casualties of the First World War

30436 Private P.H. Barter, 1st Btn Grenadier Guards. Died 24 August 1918. Memorial VD15, Mory Abbey Military Cemetery, Mory, France.

The cemetery contains 619 Commonwealth graves, 101 of which are unidentified, and 230 German graves.

102133 Corporal Joseph Cecil Budd, MM, Y41st Trench Mortar Bty, Royal Field Artillery. Died 30 July 1918, aged 23. Memorial XXVIII G16, Lijssenthoek Military Cemetery, Belgium.

The cemetery contains 10,751 graves, 833 of them French and German.

Captain Eustace Richard Allen Calthrop Cox, MC, 2nd Btn Devonshire Regiment. Enlisted 23 March 1915, aged 28. Died 18 March 1917 and believed to be buried in France

27070 Private William George Edmonds, 7th Btn Somerset Light Infantry. Died 5 April 1917, aged 33. Memorial OVIIIE5, St Sever Cemetery Extension, Rouen, France.

The cemetery extension contains 8,346 Commonwealth graves of the First World War, 10 of them unidentified, and 328 from the Second World War, 18 unidentified. There are also eight foreign nationals buried here.

Dartington Casualties of the First World War

14072 Sergeant Herbert William Hill, 2nd Btn Devonshire Regiment. Died 27 September 1918, aged 26. Memorial Panel 4, Vis-en-Artois British Cemetery, France.

The memorial bears the names of 9,821 men who have no known grave.

223530 Private John Henry Hodge, 'X' 6th Trench Mortar Bty, Royal Field Artillery. Died 21 October 1918, aged 20. Memorial ii A 11, Vadencourt British Cemetery, Maissemy, France.

The cemetery contains over 750 graves, over 200 of them unidentified.

Lieutenant Harold Plumer Kellock, North Irish Horse, attd. 13th Btn 17th Bde Royal Field Artillery. Died 6 October 1918, aged 22. Memorial IV F 19, Terlincthun British Cemetery, Wimille, France.

The cemetery contains 4,378 British and Commonwealth graves and those of over 200 other nationalities, most of them German. There are also 149 Second World War burials.

15509 Lance Corporal Wilfred Henry George Kerley, 2nd Btn Scots Guards. Died 6 November 1918, aged 21. Memorial E 8, Villers-Pol Communal Cemetery Extension, France.

The cemetery contains 119 graves, two of them unidentified. There are 74 German graves, 39 unidentified.

Dartington Casualties of the First World War

Lieutenant Hugh Miller Swears, Machine Gun Corps (Infantry). Attd 'D' Btn Tank Corps. Died 11 April 1917, aged 23. Memorial Bay 10, Arras Memorial, France. The cemetery contains 2,651 Commonwealth graves, also 30 other graves, most of them German, and seven Commonwealth Second World War graves.

The Arras Memorial commemorates the almost 35,000 servicemen from the United Kingdom, New Zealand and South Africa who have no known grave.

202985 Private F. Lock, 1st/4th Btn Devonshire Regiment. Died 9 July 1917. Memorial XIII H 13, Amara War Cemetery, Iraq. The cemetery contains 4,621 graves, 925 of them unidentified.

In 1933, all the headstones were removed when salts in the soil were causing them to deteriorate. A screen wall was erected with the names of all those buried engraved upon it.

245968 Private Frederick John Wakeham, 11th Btn Cheshire Regiment. Died 29 April 1918, aged 19. Tyne Cot Memorial, Belgium.

The largest Commonwealth war cemetery in the world in terms of burials, with 11,952 graves, 8,365 of them unidentified. The memorial bears the names of almost 35,500 men whose graves are unknown.

11964 Private John Western, 10th Btn Devonshire Regiment, Died 13 August 1917, aged 55. Memorial C541, Karasouli Military Cemetery, Greece.

The cemetery contains 1,422 Commonwealth graves of the First World War.

The Mons Star (left) *and the 1914-15 Star*

Christmas 1914 received a small brass tin containing cigarettes, pipe tobacco, chocolate and sweets. There was also a greetings card with the message, written in King George V's script, 'May God protect you and bring you home safe'.

The tin was embossed with Princess Mary's head, silhouetted in a garlanded circle, with 'Imperium Britannicum' at the top and the names of the Allies – Belgium, France, Serbia, Japan, Russia and Montenegro – around the edges.

The Second World War

On 30 January 1933 Adolf Hitler became Chancellor of the German Reich and in October of the same year withdrew from the League of Nations. In August 1934 Hitler became President and Germany began rearmament on a very large scale. Britain's biggest fear was of a gas attack on its population, and in 1938 gasmasks, including a special 'carry-bag' type for babies, were issued to every citizen, .

By June 1939, with war in Europe inevitable, men in Britain between 20 and 21 were required to register under the Military Training Act, and the Women's Land Army – formed during the First World War – was reformed. By November 3,500 had joined and by March 1943 the total had reached 58,221. On 1 September Germany invaded Poland, Hitler ignoring the Allied ultimatum to withdraw his troops.

Territorials and reservists were called up and all men between 18 and 41 were liable for conscription.

At 11.15a.m. on 3 September, for the second time in a quarter of a century, Britain declared war on Germany. France followed suit at 5p.m.

The blackout came into immediate effect. During the hours of darkness, all windows were covered by thick black blinds, curtains or blankets, with not a chink of light allowed. Police and ARP wardens often patrolled the streets to make sure the law was carried out. The sharp bawl of, 'Put that b . . . . . light out!' could occasionally be heard echoing down a dark, deserted street in the early days. Vehicle head-lights were fitted with metal hoods with slits in them, allowing only a minimum of light to shine through, and bumpers were painted white, as were roadside kerbs, the bases of lampposts and even trees. Walls of sandbags were built around important buildings for protection against bomb blast. Pale blue identity cards were issued to all citizens over 16 and all persons were required to carry a gasmask when they left home.

With imports of food necessarily regulated, much more food had to be grown at home. The use of allotments was greatly increased and people were encouraged to grow what they could in their own gardens, especially potatoes. In October, 'Dig for Victory' became one of many wartime slogans, with posters displayed everywhere. In November the 'War Savings Campaign' began, and a Red Cross Penny-a-Week Fund was begun.

From 1 January 1940, 19–27-year-old men were called-up 'for the duration of war'. This age limit was later extended to 41, which meant more and more men from the parish disappearing into the Armed Forces.

Food rationing began on 8 January, with bacon, butter, ham and sugar, while bread, fish and potatoes were left unaffected. In March meat was rationed,

Service respirator, steel helmet and pay book, 1939.

Jack James in his allotment.

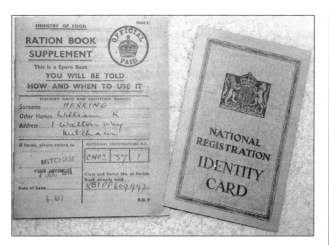

A ration book and ID card.

William 'Bill' Passmore junr (centre), *Iceland, 1940.*

Eddie Guy in his Merchant Navy uniform, 1942.

followed by tea, margarine and other fats in July, with free or cheap milk for mothers.

With the collapse of France and the threat of German invasion, an official leaflet was received in every house in Britain: 'If the invader comes – what to do and how to do it'. Church bells were silenced, to be rung only if an invasion occurred, and road signs, railway station names and milestones were removed. Long, wooden, upright poles were dug in on the large open 'prairie lands' close to Dartington Hall and Old Parsonage Farm, to deter German gliders from landing. In September, about 150 British troops, mainly Artillery with some Engineers, arrived at the hall and were billeted in the Dance School and the Chekhov Studio. Anti-aircraft guns were sited around Old Parsonage Farm, and 'double' summertime was introduced, enabling farmers to harvest in daylight later in the evenings.

The Board of Trade brought in clothes rationing on 1 June 1941, with 66 coupons allotted per person per year. A dress was 11 coupons and a gent's coat and trousers were 21. Old garments became fashionable and patches were considered patriotic! In November, points rationing on food came into force: 20 coupons per month, per person, for canned meat, fish and vegetables. Each householder was registered with a shopkeeper whose supplies were limited to the number of customers on his books. Dried milk and powdered eggs were introduced. In December, for the first time in Britain's history, unmarried women between 20 and 30 were conscripted into the Armed Forces or industry. The Red Cross Penny-a-Week Fund had amounted to over £4,000,000 in three years, over 11 million subscribers having paid in more than £50,000 every week – all in pennies! This enabled over 6,000,000 parcels to be sent to British prisoners of war.

In February 1942, food rationing was extended, an adult's ration per week being 8oz of fat, half of which was margarine, 8oz of cheese, 8oz of sugar, 4oz of ham or bacon and 1lb of meat. White bread was discontinued and replaced with an unpopular 'national wheatmeal loaf'. Bread and potatoes were the principal items for a meal – throwing away bread, or even feeding it to birds, could lead to prosecution. Chocolates, sweets and soap also went on ration, and throughout Britain, British Restaurants were set up in

William George Sercombe, RAF Regiment, pictured in September 1942.

Len Hodge, an artificer in the Royal Navy, 1943.

towns and cities where workers paid a maximum price of 5s. for a meal.

The nation was encouraged to save waste paper, scrap metal, kitchen waste (for pig food) and even bones, and were asked to contribute any loose change to 'War Weapons Week', 'Spitfire Week', 'Warship Week', etc., throughout the war years.

In November, church bells were rung to celebrate the British victory at El Alamein. During December points rationing was again extended.

German aircraft frequently passed high over the parish on night raids to Bristol or South Wales, with the occasional bomb (if any were left over) jettisoned randomly on the way back. During one such incident, a lone aircraft dropped a bomb which, landing in a field near houses in Laburnum Grove, Clay Lane, failed to explode and was found by a farmer the following morning when he went to collect his cattle. The area was sealed off while Royal Engineers defused and dug it out, and for several weeks the large green bomb casing was used to make collections for the war effort at the entrance to Totnes Pannier Market. In another incident there was slight blast damage to houses in Puddavine Terrace when a bomb exploded in a nearby orchard.

By 17 September 1944, with the war ebbing further from our shores and Allied Forces pushing the enemy back across France and Belgium, some blackout restrictions were lifted and double summer-time ended.

When the war ended in 1945, the demobilised forces were divided into two classes. Class B, which was given priority, consisted of trade workers, builders, carpenters, etc., who were urgently required for reconstruction work in Britain. Class A forces were demobbed according to age and length of service: two months' service was equivalent to a year in age, so that a serviceman of 22 with four years' service had the same release date as a man of 40 with one year's service. The first demob group was on 18 June and, by the end of the year, 750,000 men were back in civvy street. Every serviceman was given a 'demob suit' of his choice, with shirts, tie, hat, a pair of shoes and an overcoat.

The parish celebrated with a bonfire (with an effigy of Hitler on top) and sports on Foxhole playing-field. Servicemen from the parish began to return home, including Eric Clark, a prisoner of war since 1940 in Germany and Poland, and Ron Denham, who had been a PoW in Germany. With the surrender of Japan in August 1945, Tom Webber, a Royal Marine who had survived the sinking of HMS *Repulse* in December 1941 only to suffer as a prisoner of war under the Japanese for nearly four years, returned home, as did Stan Dingle, a Burma campaign veteran.

A total of 60,585 civilians were killed by enemy bombing in Britain during the war.

Although hostilities had ended, bread remained on ration until 1948, to help feed the millions of starving people throughout Europe and Asia. Clothes came off ration in 1949, milk, eggs, flour and canned goods in 1950, tea in 1952, sweets and chocolate in February 1953 and, finally, meat, on 3 July 1954. After almost 15 years, rationing had come to an end!

Edgar Hodge (right) *and Neil Harding, RAF, 1944.*

From left, *the 1939–45 Star, the Defence Medal and the War Medal.*

Dartington Hall Estate Workers who lost their lives in the Second World War

Kevin Black	School pupil	Army
J. Blake	Marley Fruit Farm	RAC
C. I. Clements	Staverton Builders	Army
J. Corkhill	School pupil	Fleet Air Arm
H.G. Craigmile	Central Office	RAF
Terry Gilbert	Farms	Army
R.A. Hanks	Sawmills	RAF
W. Hunter	School	RAF
W.F. Kerswell	Farms	Army
J. McGhey	Staverton Builders	RAF
J. Pulford	Woodlands	RAF
A. Tapper	Sawmills	RN
K.C. Walton	School	RAF
C. Williams-Ellis	School pupil	Army

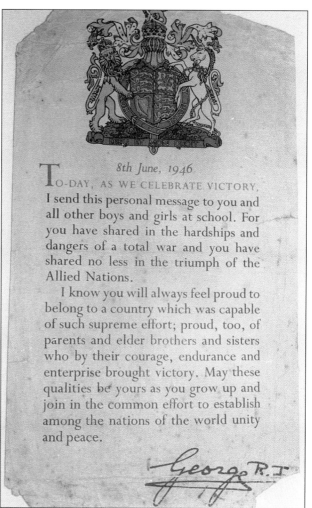

8th June, 1946

TO-DAY, AS WE CELEBRATE VICTORY, I send this personal message to you and all other boys and girls at school. For you have shared in the hardships and dangers of a total war and you have shared no less in the triumph of the Allied Nations.

I know you will always feel proud to belong to a country which was capable of such supreme effort; proud, too, of parents and elder brothers and sisters who by their courage, endurance and enterprise brought victory. May these qualities be yours as you grow up and join in the common effort to establish among the nations of the world unity and peace.

George R.I

The scroll presented to schoolchildren in June 1946.

Wartime Evacuees

The evacuation of civilians (most of them children) during the war years was in three phases. During July and August 1939, with the threat of hostilities getting closer, rehearsals took place in London of the evacuation of hundreds of children from the capital for fear of mass enemy bombing.

When war was declared on 3 September 1939, these plans were immediately put into operation. During the following weeks 827,000 schoolchildren, 524,000 pre-school children and mothers, 12,000 pregnant mothers and 103,000 teachers and helpers were evacuated to Essex, Suffolk and Norfolk. When the expected bombing failed to materialise, most had returned to their homes by Christmas.

The largest evacuation was in the summer and autumn of 1940, when the occupation of France, Belgium and Holland brought enemy bombers much closer to our shores. The government initiated a scheme for children to be sent abroad, 70,000 being sent overseas, most to Canada and America, while others went to South Africa and Australia. The scheme was suspended in September 1940, after the

Dartington Casualties of the Second World War

D/KX 95221 Ralph Fernley Arscott, Stoker 1st Class, HMS Galatea (cruiser). Died 14 December 1941. Panel 52, Column 2, Plymouth Naval Memorial.

The memorial commemorates 23,183 sailors who sailed from Plymouth and were lost at sea, over 7,000 in the First World War and almost 16,000 in the Second World War. HMS Galatea was torpedoed by U-557 outside Alexandria harbour when returning from a patrol in the Mediterranean.

Lieutenant Richard John Chavasse Holder, Dorset Regiment. Attd 4th PWO Gurkha Rifles. Died 14 March 1944, aged 23.

Location of grave unknown.

651127 Sergeant William Hunter, 37 Sqdn Royal Air Force. Died 3 April 1945. Panel 18, Column 2, Malta Memorial.

The Malta Memorial commemorates the 2,298 Commonwealth airmen who lost their lives in operations around the Mediterranean and who have no known grave.

5623423 Corporal William Frank Kerswell, 2/6th Btn The Queen's Royal Regiment (West Surrey). Died 22 February 1944, aged 24. Memorial XXC3, Beach Head War Cemetery, Anzio, Italy.

The cemetery contains 2,312 Commonwealth graves, 291 of them unidentified. There is also one First World War burial.

Dartington Casualties of the Second World War

1407478 Leading Aircraftman William George Sercombe, Royal Air Force Volunteer Reserve. Died 23 August 1944, aged 22. Memorial IV K 19, Ancona War Cemetery, Italy.

The cemetery contains 1,019 Commonwealth graves, 55 of them unidentified.

1182873 Warrant Officer Graham Campbell Stafford, DFM, Royal Air Force Volunteer Reserve. Died 4 April 1943. Memorial Panel 134, Runnymede Memorial, Surrey.

The Air Forces Memorial commemorates the 20,339 airmen lost during operations from Britain and Europe who have no known grave.

649374 Flight Sergeant Kennedy Charles Walton, 18 Sqdn Royal Air Force. Died 11 April 1941, aged 20. Memorial Panel 38, Runnymede Memorial, Surrey.

The memorial commemorates 20,339 airmen from Britain, the Commonwealth and European countries, who served in the Royal Air Force during the Second World War and have no known grave.

D/J 87186 Able Seaman Henry Couch Williams, HMS Jupiter (Destroyer) Died 27 February 1942, aged 40. Memorial Panel 67 Column 1, Plymouth Naval Memorial.

The memorial commemorates 23,183 sailors who sailed from Plymouth and were lost at sea, over 7,000 in the First World War and almost 16,000 in the Second World War. HMS Jupiter was blown up by a mine in the Java Sea during operations against Japanese Naval Forces.

Evacuees paddle in the Dart in the summer of 1941.

liner *City of Benares* was torpedoed and sank with the loss of 77 children and 170 adults and crew.

The third phase of evacuation, on a smaller scale, was from June to September 1944, when the Germans launched their V1 (doodlebug) and V2 rocket attacks on London and the South East. These gradually ceased as the launching sites were captured by advancing Allied Forces.

Dartington Evacuees

In January 1939, with the likelihood of war getting closer, preparations were begun in the village for the reception of evacuees and the parish was surveyed for accommodation. The area was divided into 11 districts, each containing about 25 houses, and authorised visitors were appointed to call on householders and ascertain the accommodation available on a voluntary basis.

With the outbreak of war in September, when this information was brought up to date, Dartington was prepared to accommodate nearly 200 children. Of these, 80 were to be housed, more or less temporarily, in certain large rooms at Dartington Hall and in the youth hostel at Lownard, while the remainder were to be billeted in private homes. These numbers were calculated on the assumption that each child would be accompanied by its mother.

The German invasion of France and the Low Countries in May 1940 had an immediate effect on Dartington Hall School. All teachers of German nationality, and some pupils, were interned without notice, and about 60–70 children were removed by their parents. At this time negotiations were going on with the London County Council for the letting of the Junior School buildings for the duration of the war. It was therefore decided to concentrate both Junior and Senior Schools at Foxhole, leaving the three boarding houses and the Junior School empty. When this move took place, all the equipment, crockery, blankets and teaching materials went too, leaving the buildings bare.

Towards the end of May, Dartington was notified that 357 children had been allotted to them under the new plan for evacuation. They were told that it was essential to be prepared for the maximum number and that the first trainload to arrive in Totnes Rural District would be taken to Dartington. Careful scrutiny of the lists showed that, even with the utmost goodwill of the parish, it would not be possible to billet more than 200 children in private houses, and that the new compulsory powers might have to be employed. It was clear, therefore, that about 150 children would have to be communally housed and the Dartington Hall Trustees' offer of the Dance School building for this purpose was gladly accepted. Plans for the opening of a children's hostel were put in hand by Helen Elmhirst and Ruth Martin.

In June 1940, over 160,000 schoolchildren were evacuated from London and the South East to safer areas in the South West, the Midlands and Wales.

The grave of evacuee Dennis Morgan, who drowned in the River Dart.

Each child wore a name label on their coat lapel and carried a gasmask in a cardboard case hung over a shoulder, with a few items of clothing or personal belongings in a parcel, small suitcase or haversack. A few possessed only the clothing they wore.

In the early morning of Friday, 14 June, a special train left Gravesend, Kent, bound for Totnes, via Waterloo, with 134 children and their teachers from Westcourt and Whitehill Schools. At Waterloo Station they were joined by another 400 children, with 30 teachers and helpers, from two LCC Schools, Friars and Southwark. The children were aged between three and 14, and some children simply turned up at Waterloo and had to be taken along. This caused many more children to be taken to Totnes than was intended. Roger Morel, the billeting officer from Dartington, and his helpers, met them at

Totnes Station. They were transported by bus, some to Dartington Hall, others to the Village Hall, where householders collected their new 'family' member(s). On 19 October an additional 100 London evacuees arrived in the village.

Householders who took in a child under 14 were granted a weekly allowance of 3s., while 5s. was allowed for an adult or a child over 14.

Tragedy struck in 1941 when, on 14 June, 8-year-old orphan Dennis Morgan, an evacuee from Gravesend whose grandparents were his guardians, was drowned in the River Dart. He was buried in Dartington churchyard on 21 June.

More evacuees arrived from Plymouth and Bristol during 1941, when the cities were targeted by German bombers. During the next 4¹⁄₂ years some, their mothers wanting them back, returned home, while others stayed until they were of school-leaving age (14 at that time).

When the war with Germany ended in May 1945, the evacuees returned home, the last to leave Dartington, on 24 June, being four mothers and 15 children whose parents had not been traced or who had no home to return to. They were transferred to a hostel at Harberton. A few wished to remain with their 'foster' mums and settled in the village.

The Home Guard, 1940–44

In October 1939, Winston Churchill proposed that a 'Home Guard' of 500,000 men' over the age of 40 should be formed.

The German airborne invasion of Belgium and Holland on 10 May 1940 focused attention on the use of paratroops dropped behind enemy lines, and it was thought highly probable that these would be used during an invasion of England. On 14 May,

Dartington Home Guard in the 1940s. Left to right, back row: *Noel Wakeham, Paddy O'Harahan, Eddie Prout, Jack James, Hugh Fowler, Ernest Clake, ? Walter Thomas, Jack Last, Clifford Cordy, William Pook, William Ambrose, Walter Harris, Stanley Ivey;* middle row: *Henry Rogers, Tom Dance, Bert Helbes (Sgt), Victor Syms, ? Hines, Tom Blight, Dennis Martin, Jim Head, Harry Doidge, Reg Denham, Dei MacTaggart, Maurice Clements;* front row: *Harry Walters, Dick Legg, Frank Barnes, Jim Taylor, Jim Martin, Charlie Winson, Clarence Miller, Richard King.*

Dartington Home Guard in the 1940s, with Reg Newson (back row, fifth from left).

Anthony Eden, Secretary of State for War, broadcast an appeal for British male subjects between the ages of 17 and 65 to join a military organisation, the 'Local Defence Volunteers' (LDV). Enlistment forms (AFW3066) were sent out and, by 20 May, nearly 250,000 men had volunteered. By the end of the month this figure had grown to 300,000, including ex-servicemen and First World War veterans.

The immediate problem was a shortage of uniforms, arms and equipment, and until the end of July, the volunteers wore denims, forage caps and an LDV armlet on their right arm, while 'weapons' for drill often consisted of broomsticks, muskets and shotguns, with a few old US Enfield .30 M1917 rifles for guard duties.

On 31 July the LDV became the Home Guard. Eventually, battledress was issued, the various equipment, steel helmets, respirators, boots, webbing ammunition pouches and leather gaiters being specially produced for the Home Guard. Gradually, men were armed with the standard Lee Enfield 3.03 rifle and bayonet.

Devon was divided into four zones: North, South, East and Plymouth, each city, town and village having its contingent. By September, Dartington Home Guard had 70 members, their headquarters being in stone buildings at Shinner's Bridge, with the nearby disused quarry used as a rifle-range. The area they defended was bounded by the River Dart from Weir Head to Hood Bridge, then across country to Tigley and back along the railway line to Malt Bridge, its salient features being the river crossings and the strategic road junction at Shinner's Bridge.

Germany's invasion of England, planned for 15 September, was postponed and, ultimately, never happened.

In October, Home Guard volunteers were granted a subsistence allowance: 1s.6d. for a five-hour shift and 3s. for an eight-hour 'turn'. By the end of the year, Devon had 20 battalions.

In January 1941, 'Home Guard' shoulder titles were issued, with a square patch underneath with the inscription 'DVN' and battalion number.

In February 1942, despite the threat of German invasion being over, compulsory service was introduced for certain categories of men, with 24 hours' training every four weeks. 'Private' replaced the title 'Volunteer' and, during 1942, the Sten gun, a semi-automatic weapon used for close-quarter street fighting, was issued – it was said to have cost 7s.6d. to make!

By 1943 there were 1,100 Home Guard battalions in Britain, with a total of 1.75 million men. Many 17-year-olds served in its ranks before their call-up into the regular forces.

In September 1944, with Allied Forces pushing across France and into Belgium and Holland, no further men were directed into the Home Guard.

Begun on 1 November, the order to 'Stand down' was completed on 31 December. On 3 December 7,000 members from every part of the country took part in a final parade in London, where King George VI took the salute in Hyde Park. 'Dad's Army', after four years, had come to an end!

The Americans Arrive, 1942–44

On 26 January 1942, the US 34th Infantry Division disembarked at Belfast, Northern Ireland. The first American troops to land in Britain since 1917, at that time they were still equipped with British-style steel helmets.

That October, the US 29th Infantry Division, on board the liner *Queen Mary*, docked at Gourock in Scotland before progressing to Tidworth, Wiltshire.

In May 1943, the Division arrived in Devon, setting up their headquarters at Tavistock, with the 121st Engineer Combat Battalion at Paignton, the

175th Regimental Combat Team at Torquay and Exeter, the 116th Regimental Combat at Ivybridge and the 227th Field Artillery at Okehampton.

In the summer of 1943, US naval bases were established at Appledore and Instow, North Devon.

The first Americans to arrive in the village only stayed about six weeks and were billeted in the Dance School and Chekhov Studio, previously occupied by British troops, at Dartington Hall. Owing to the limited room in the hall's White Hart Club, a bar and recreation room first converted from service rooms in the 1930s, only officers and sergeants were allowed to join, though privates could be 'signed in' by a full member. On the first evening, five sergeants enjoyed themselves so much that they were late returning to their billet and were subsequently reduced to privates, thereafter becoming known as 'the unholy five'!

Shortly after the unit left, black American soldiers arrived. Staying for about three weeks, they were reported to be well behaved, and their sergeants were also allowed access to the White Hart Club.

On 16 August 1943 the first landing exercise took place on Slapton Sands to test its suitability as a future training area. 'M' Company and HQ Company of the 175th US Combat Team embarked from Dartmouth in Royal Navy landing craft.

In September 1943 the Assault Training Centre (ATC) was set up at Woolacombe Sands to train US combat teams to attack specially built replica German concrete emplacements. Most American soldiers had no combat or amphibious experience, nor the special skills needed to attack large fortified German coastal positions along the 'Atlantic Wall'. The US 156th Infantry Division provided most of the training staff. Having completed a two- or three-week course, regiments then took part in the large Corps landings on the Battle Training Area at Slapton Sands.

On 29 September 1,930 men of US Naval Construction Battalion (SEABEEs) arrived in Salcombe to set up United States Naval-Advanced Amphibious Base (USN-AAB). Eventually, the force outnumbered the civilian population.

In October 1943 E. Richards of 'C' Company, US 392nd Engineers, stationed in Ivybridge, was court-martialled at Dartington for disposing of US petrol to a civilian. Sentenced to six months' hard labour, he forfeited two-thirds of his pay for six months.

The US 5th Engineer Regiment (mainly black GIs), along with the civilian workforce, were employed on the site of the former Totnes racecourse, building landing-craft and Bailey bridges. Afro-American GIs were segregated into all-black units (mainly transport and engineer), usually with white officers. Relations between blacks and whites were not cordial and there were frequent fights, sometimes with knives.

While many white GIs disliked their fellow countrymen simply because of their colour, most British people found this strange, and accepted black Americans into their homes, pubs, cinemas, shops, etc. After all, they were in the same Army and fighting the same enemy! US military authorities put some towns out of bounds to off-duty personnel, only allowing white and black GIs to enter on alternate days and nights, to avoid confrontation. Dances were never held for black and white GIs together. It was not until the Korean War (1950–53) that US regiments became mixed.

On 4 November 1943 an area of 25 square miles around Slapton Sands was evacuated of all civilians, livestock and farm equipment, for use as an American training area.

On 8 November 1943, 34,142 men and 3,306 vehicles of the US 1st Infantry Division docked at Liverpool. Known as the 'Big Red One', the Division symbol being a large '1' on a dark green shield, they headed for camps in Dorset. The Division had already seen action in North Africa in November 1942, had fought in Tunisia and had taken part in the invasion of Sicily in July 1943.

On the same day a very large USN-AAB was established at Plymouth.

On 12 November 1943, HQ American Forces invited villagers to a dance held in the Dance School hall, with music provided by an RAF band.

On 16 November 1943 the evacuation began of 3,000 people from seven parishes around Slapton Sands, and was completed in six weeks, .

On 22 November 1943, USN-AAB (3,684 men) was established at Dartmouth/Kingswear. A small naval base was set up at Teignmouth, a store at Tiverton and at Exeter the largest store in Britain, covering 95 acres, with 2,352 American naval personnel, was established.

During November, the US 29th Infantry Division moved into Cornwall and the Plymouth area.

On 20 December 1943, with the evacuation of Slapton Sands area complete, it was handed over to the American military authority.

From 31 December 1943 to 2 January 1944, Exercise 'Duck', Force 'U', US 29th Infantry Division, embarked from Falmouth, landing on Slapton Sands. The 'enemy' opposing them were paratroopers from the 101st US Airborne Division.

On 18 January 1944 the US 4th Infantry Division, known as the 'Ivy Boys', their Division sign being four ivy leaves with the Roman numerals IV, sailed from New York, disembarking 11 days later at Liverpool and travelling by rail to Devon. Headquarters were set up at Collipriest Tiverton, along with Divisional Signals and the reconnaissance unit. The 42nd Field Artillery were based at Broomhill Camp, Honiton, with the 44th Field Artillery at Denbury Camp, near Newton Abbot, and the 4th Quartermaster Company and 704th Ordnance Company at Exeter. From 1253 US Combat Engineers, 800 men travelled by train from Bristol to

Dorothy Elmhirst with personnel of the 4th US Infantry Division in early 1944.

Totnes. Billeted at Dartington Hall, they practised building Bailey bridges across the River Dart.

On 1 February 1944, 25 GIs, the advance party from Falmouth HQ, arrived at Kingston House, Staverton, to establish Area 'K' Signal Depot; eventually 360 men were billeted there.

Engineers constructed a concrete deep-water tank-testing pool at Shinner's Bridge, on waste ground next to Bidwell Brook. When completed, convoys of Sherman tanks stretched back for miles along the Plymouth (A385) road, with Scammell tank transporters lined up along the Buckfastleigh (A384) road. Each five-man crew would waterproof their tank with a 'gunk'-like substance and proceed down the ramp and through the water before being winched up onto a transporter. A few months after D-Day, council workmen drained this pool, breaking up the base and filling it in. The ramps and sides still remain.

Throughout spring, the build-up of the US 1st Army continued. The 1st Infantry Division 5th Corps, who led the assault on Omaha Beach, were in Dorset; the 4th Infantry Division 7th Corps, the assault troops for Utah Beach, in South Devon, and the 29th Infantry Division 5th Corps, follow-up troops for Omaha, in the Plymouth area and Cornwall. Other divisions were in South Wales.

About one and a quarter million US servicemen were stationed throughout the West Country – Devon was said to be the most military county in Britain. American vehicles were everywhere, all with the large white star insignia on them, their drivers learning to stay on the left and negotiate the narrow Devonshire lanes – not an easy task with a 30-ton Sherman tank (length 19ft 6ins, width 9ft, height 9ft 3ins), or a 31ft long amphibian DUKW. Many a time stone walls were damaged and road surfaces torn up on corners, where tanks and tracked vehicles swivelled around.

Passing GIs would often throw 'K' rations (a sealed waterproof pack 10ins x 4ins) to locals, containing biscuits, chocolate, candy, chewing-gum, and cigarettes, usually Lucky Strikes or Camels.

The Americans never appeared to be short of food supplies, which were shipped over from the States, and were sympathetic to our meagre wartime rationing, often parting with tins of beans, butter, ground coffee, frankfurters, peanut butter, sausages, sweetcorn, apricots, peaches, pears, pineapples, coke – some items we hadn't seen for over four years. You name it, the Yanks had it – always in tins! They also introduced the British to jazz and jitterbugging, and to such tunes as 'In the Mood', 'String of Pearls', 'Moonlight Serenade' and 'Tuxedo Junction', as well as to nylon stockings and silk undies – favourites with the ladies!

Disaster struck in the early hours of 28 April 1944 during exercise 'Tiger', when a convoy of eight LSTs, loaded with men and vehicles heading for the Slapton Sands training area, were attacked in Lyme Bay by nine German E-boats. Two LSTs were torpedoed and sunk and a third, badly damaged, limped into Dartmouth. The loss of 946 American soldiers and sailors was a severe blow. Being so close to D-Day, however, it was quickly hushed-up and was kept secret for a number of years, even after the war had ended.

Although 1 May 1944 was the planned initial date for D-Day, this was later postponed until 5 June, preparations for the assault on Normandy being not quite ready.

From 3 to 6 May, 'Fabius' the last exercise on Slapton Sands, took place: Force 'O', US 1st Infantry Division, sailed from Portland and Poole. The 'Big Red One' were to suffer heavy losses a month later in the assault on Omaha Beach.

On 16 May, units moved out from their regular camps into special marshalling areas, mostly tented, in fields which stretched along the main roads leading to the embarkation ports, columns of vehicles being lined up and camouflaged. The areas were known as 'sausages' and letter coded, South Brent,

Dartington and Totnes 'K', East Plymouth, Ivybridge and Kitley 'L', West Plymouth and Cornwall 'M'.

On 26 May the marshalling areas were sealed off and the troops put under strict security, with civilian contact forbidden, while the main roads, except those with special authority, were closed to traffic. The sudden absence of GIs from shops, pubs, cinemas and streets alerted the public that something was imminent; and they didn't have long to wait!

Suddenly, on 2 and 3 June, the whole of the US 1st Army was on the move – and there were no final goodbyes. The 25,000 troops and 2,750 vehicles of the 4th Infantry Division moved to their embarkation ports – Torquay, Brixham and Dartmouth. The 29th Infantry Division moved to Plymouth, Saltash and Falmouth, and the 1st Infantry Division to Portland, Poole and Weymouth. On 4 June, the convoys sailed for the assembly area. The next day, owing to bad weather, the invasion was postponed for 24 hours. The troops, many of them sea-sick, remained on board their landing craft and ships.

On 6 June, D-Day, of the 156,000 troops who landed on the Normandy coast by sea and air, about 10,000 were killed, wounded or reported missing, fewer casualties than was expected.

With the GIs gone, it was quiet around the village. There were rows of empty tents, with only the occasional American vehicle as rear parties recovered the gear and cleared the sites before joining their comrades in Normandy. In July, American Engineers began clearing barbed wire, mines, ammunition, etc., from Slapton Training Area, before residents could begin to return to their villages and farms in the autumn. The USN-AAB at Dartmouth closed.

During the last six months of the year, American activity continued in the Dorset area and, after training on Salisbury Plain, a number of infantry and armoured divisions sailed to France from Portland and Weymouth.

When the European war ended in May 1945, the USN-AAB at Salcombe closed and in September the only one remaining, that in Plymouth, also closed.

About 70,000 British girls married US servicemen and in February 1946, the first GI brides, with their children, sailed on the *Queen Mary* to join their husbands in the States.

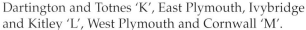

American GI Jargon, 1943–44

AR's	*Army regulations*
Bird Colonel	*Full Colonel*
Buzz	*To fly low*
Chow Hound	*Man fond of eating*
Chow Line	*Mess queue*
Dog face	*Infantry soldier*
Draftee	*Conscript*
Duck	*Amphibious vehicle*
First John	*First Lieutenant*
French bath	*Washing in a GI steel helmet*
Funny money	*Sterling (£ s d)*
Furlough	*Leave*
GI/Joe	*US soldier*
GI Jane	*US Women's Auxiliary Army Corps*
Hash mark	*Service stripe*
Holy Joe	*Chaplain*
Kraut	*German*
Latrine	*Toilets*
Latrine Lawyer	*Barracks Lawyer*
Maggie's drawers	*Red flag waved on a rifle range*
Milk run	*Easy job*
Night fighter	*Negro GI*
Over the hill	*AWOL (Absent while on leave)*
Piccadilly commando	*Prostitute*
Red-lined	*Cancelled*
Re-tread	*Old officer recalled for active service*
Sack	*Bed*
Shack job	*Easy woman*
Shack-up	*To sleep with a woman*
Shipping out	*Departing*
Shortarm	*VD inspection*
Sky Pilot	*Chaplain*
Snowball/Snowdrop	*US Military Policeman*
Son of a bitch	*No good*
Step-ins	*Panties*
Top kick	*First Sargeant*
Zied	*Sent home i.e. America.*

RAF Rehabilitation Scheme, Dartington, 1944

Set up by Dorothy Elmhirst in the latter years of the war, the scheme *(see below)* enabled airmen from the Queen Victoria Hospital, East Grinstead, who had

Flight Lieutenant Craig	*2–9 June*	*Woodlands*
Flying Officer A.A. 'Jimmy' Barrow	*2–7 August*	*Gardens*
Sergeant R. Major	*2 June–21 July*	*Farms*
Flying Officer Stanley, aged 32	*23 June–23 September*	*Sawmills*
Flight Sergeant Dennis Smith, aged 20 , Pilot	*28 June–28 August*	*Farms*
Warrant Officer Wilson, aged 20, Aircrew	*28 June–1 September*	*Forestry*
Flight Sergeant David Bond, aged 20, Observer	*12 July – October*	*Farm and Forestry*
Leading Aircraftman G. 'Ginger' Warne, aged 30, Ground Crew	*12 July – October*	*Farms*
Warrant Officer H. Halahan , aged 33	*23 July–23 September*	*Woodlands*
Warrant Officer S. F. C. Powell, aged 24, Pilot	*July ?*	

suffered burns and disfigurement, to come for a maximum of three months to work on the estate to help them readjust to life. They chose which department they would like to work in and how long they stayed. Some found it interesting, while others found it difficult to adapt to the work and environment.

The first three arrived on 2 June 1944, and were met at Totnes Station.

Dartington Hall Fire Brigade, 1941–53

In 1941 Dartington Hall formed its own fire brigade, with a lorry and water pump painted in wartime NFS grey, and employees as trained firemen. It carried on after the war until disbanded in 1953.

Fireman Frank Lake.

Dartington Hall firemen on parade, late 1940.s. The Fire Chief is Richard 'Dick' Rushton.

Fireman Edgar Hodge.

National Service memorabilia.

Cousins Mike (left: 43LAA/SL Regt RA) and William (76 HAA Regt RA) MacLening, April 1953.

The author on coronation duty, London, June 1953.

CHAPTER 6

National Service

'We also served.'

Between 1947 and 1960 many young men from the village were called up for National Service.

On three occasions during the last century, 1916, 1939 and 1947, Britain had resorted to compulsory military service, for men over the age of 18. Over 14 million men were 'called-up' to serve in the armed forces from 1916 to 1961.

The post-war National Service Act, introduced in March 1947, became law in May, making liable for compulsory military service every male citizen between the ages of 18 and 26. Those serving an apprenticeship were deferred until the age of 21. Enlistment always took place on a Thursday. Exemption was granted to agricultural workers, coalminers, clergymen, merchant seamen, police cadets, science teachers and seagoing fishermen.

In 1947 conscripts served for one year, with six years as a Reservist, but within a year these periods were increased to 18 months and four years, and on

'Bram' Bartlett, RAF.

Barrack room kit lay-out during the years of National Service. Lay-outs varied with each regiment.

National Service Medal, 1939–60.

Brian 'Bill' Tuffnell, RAF.

Brian Tuffnell in Egypt.

The author on his twentieth birthday, October 1954, ready for 24-hour guard duty.

Stanley Quaintance, Royal Artillery.

31 August 1950, after the Korean War started, to two years and 5½ years reserve.

From 5 April 1957 National Service was progressively reduced until 1961, after which no further conscripts were called up. By April 1963, only the Army retained 2,600 National Servicemen and, on 13 May 1963, the last conscript was demobbed; thus all the Services were once again made up solely of regulars. Of the Armed Forces, the Army gained most from conscription, its annual intake of around 160,000 men, bringing its strength from 380,000 in 1949 to 440,000 by 1953. National Servicemen made up 50 per cent of the Army's total manpower – in many regiments the figure was over 50 per cent. A total of 1,132,872 conscripts served in the British Army, which claimed 33 per cent of all conscripts, with the Air Force claiming 12 per cent and the Navy, which preferred volunteers for long-term engagements, only 10 per cent.

In all, 395 National Servicemen gave their lives.

There is a National Service Memorial at Alrewes, Staffordshire. The last Sunday in June each year is designated as National Service Day.

Shinner's Bridge Farm: 1925.

Shinner's Bridge from Cott Road, c.1960.

CHAPTER 7

Around the Parish

Shinner's Bridge

Now the hub of the village, in 70 years Shinner's Bridge has changed from a once typical Devon village crossroads to a roundabout, surrounded by new developments, often with traffic bumper to bumper, especially at peak times. The winding road to Totnes remains the same as when constructed in the early-nineteenth century, and struggles to cope with today's volume of traffic. The road from Shinner's Bridge to Marley Head, opened as a turn-pike road in the 1830s, was once the route of both the Torquay to Plymouth Devon General Omnibus Co. and of the Western National, while only Western National buses used the A384 to Buckfastleigh.

It was here that, in 1835, Miss Spedding, sister-in-law to the rector, Archdeacon Froude, had four tene-ments, or almshouses, built for poor persons of the village, who lived rent free. Water was supplied via a pump in the front garden. In 1911, one of the houses was occupied by the district nurse, who paid a yearly rent of £1.

In September 1912, a sub-Post Office was opened at No. 1 Shinner's Bridge Cottages, with Mrs Jane Pearce as postmistress. It was run by Mrs Sarah 'Nellie' Almond from 1919 until the late 1920s, when the new grocery store was built, taking over the role of Post Office. The only shop in the village, it was run by the Guy family for many years.

The once open ground, now reduced in size, where in bygone years a steamroller and its caravan would park overnight when road resurfacing in the area, has been grassed over, with seating along the pathway. In 1953, three local primary school children, Gwen Denham, Denise Sutcliffe and Peter Clake, planted three cherry trees here to commemo-rate the Queen's coronation.

The Cider Press Centre, once the cider mill and originally a farm, attracts visitors from far and wide. On sale here are Dartington glass, household wares, books, etc; and passing coach parties often stop here for a welcome cup of tea in Cranks restaurant.

The village Primary School has expanded to cope with the growing population, and Bidwell Brook, a special needs school, has been built close by. The Meadowbrook Centre, opened in 1969, and a popular venue for social events, receptions, reunions, etc., has an adjoining swimming pool. 'Robins', a respite and life-skills centre, is another added development.

The grocery store/Post Office has been altered over the years, as has the adjoining service station.

The former Central Office building is now called the Lescaze Centre (named after the architect who designed it). Opposite is the Dorothy Elmhirst Playing-field, home to one of the local football clubs and a venue for local events.

The Central/Lescaze Office

Designed by William Lescaze, the building opened in 1935 as administrative offices, laboratories and a library for the Dartington Hall Trust, and in 1947 the Adult Education Centre was opened, teaching a variety of crafts.

Now known as the Lescaze Offices, it has under-gone additions and alterations over the years and is now rented out by the Trust.

Cott Cross Cottage

Now called Bluebell Cottage, Cott Cross Cottage was the home of the author for 16 years and of his parents for over 45 years, from May 1940 to January 1986. Originally two cottages, George Tucker, the landlord, and his family lived in one until the building was converted into a single dwelling by the author's father when he purchased both properties in November 1959.

A fourteenth-century thatched cottage, its 'cob' walls, a mixture of clay, chopped straw, horsehair and stone, are about 3ft thick. During decorating in May 1983, behind several layers of wallpaper above a bedroom door, the inscription, 'Pax Intrantibus' (Peace to the Traveller) was uncovered, suggesting that the cottage may have been an overspill for the

Painting of Cott Cottage by schoolteacher Tom Blight, 1943.

Cott Cross Cottage, 1940.

Audrey, Edward, William, and Mike MacLening with evacuee Richard, Cott Cross, 1941.

The author with evacuee Richard Ludlow, summer 1941.

The author in 1949.

Cott Inn when it was a staging post. Many years ago, according to an elderly local, one of the upstairs rooms was once used as a classroom, the wooden pegs along one wall being where the children hung their hats and coats. A blocked-up side window may have resulted from a Window Tax, imposed in 1695.

We moved in on 9 May 1940, taking over the tenancy from two elderly sisters. Conditions in the cottage were quite primitive, accommodation being a single room downstairs and two bedrooms. Access was by a low front door only and, with no electricity, a gas lamp in the centre of the living-room provided light, while cooking (and heating) was done on a large black stove with oven, or a small gasring.

Water was drawn from an outside tap beside a stone trough in the cobbled front yard, dirty water being taken out to a drain. On bath night a tin bath in front of the fire was filled with water heated in kettles and saucepans, the bath being afterwards carried outside to be emptied. The only toilet was a large 'Elsan'

The author with his wife Betty and daughter Judith, Cott Cross, August 1957.

Afternoon tea, with William and Tessa MacLening and their Aunty Claire at Cott Cross in the 1970s.

The author's family, July 1979. From left: father 'Jeff', wife Betty, mother Claire, daughter Judith and son Paul.

bucket in a dilapidated wooden shed next to the coal-shed at the rear of the cottage, which was emptied into a deep hole dug in the garden. Father replaced it with a brick-built structure before being called-up for war service a few months later.

In June 1940, Richard Ludlow, an evacuee from Gravesend a couple of years older than me, joined us. On 5 November my mother's eldest sister and her family (six children aged 10 years to 1 month), plus their black labrador dog, arrived, having been evacuated from Kent. Eight young children, two adults and two dogs in a two bedroomed cottage! Seating at mealtimes consisted of a wooden plank supported by chairs at either end of the table, while the two mothers sat one at each end. Sleeping arrangements consisted of a double bed in the small bedroom with two girls at the top and three boys at the bottom, while the two mothers slept in a double bed in the larger bedroom, with Richard and I top to tail in a canvas camp bed and the baby in a drawer. Bath nights were split over Saturday and Sunday – no time for modesty! We lived (and survived) in those conditions for three or four months, until the 'Macs' moved into accommodation in the annexe at 'Dawn', now a residential home.

In 1942, when the small leaded landing window was blown in by the blast from a German bomb dropped at Puddaven, a larger paned window replaced it.

An indoor water tap and sink, electricity and a flush toilet were installed a few years after the war and the cobbled yard was concreted over. The large stone boulder against the boundary wall, often moved out of position by the tracks of American Sherman tanks when they negotiated the corner during 1943/44, still remains.

Village Scenes

Forder Lane cottages in the 1800s.

'Lostwithiel', Cott Road, August 1929. On the right *is the Devon Constabulary police house, for many years the home of the village bobby.*

Village Scenes

Droridge farmhouse, 2005.

'Smithfield', Cott Road, originally a farmhouse: 1930/40's.

Village Scenes

'Ailbins', Cott Lane, c.1960...

... and in about 1990.

Village Scenes

Left: *The Smithy, 1903, ..and* (below) *in 2006, almost a century later.*

Village Scenes

Puddaven Cottages, c.1900.

Puddaven Cottages in the 1930s. Note the sign on the wall, offering camping and bed and breakfast.

Village Scenes

Puddaven Cottages in the 1950s.

Cott Court cottages in 2004. These were originally thatched.

Village Scenes

Week House, 1905. Originally a farmhouse, it was then converted into a pub, the Champernowne Arms, but after a few years was restored to a farmhouse again.

Thatched cottages at Week, c.1930.

Village Scenes

C. Miller at Week, c.1920.

The former YMCA youth hostel, Lownard, Week.

Hammercott Hole

Hammercott Hole, situated beside Droridge Lane between Crossing Cross and Redlake Cross, is named after a stonemason who, in 1878, was working on the building of the church. He had been quenching his thirst in the Cott Inn and apparently stumbled into the hole on his way home. Trapped overnight, he was rescued the next morning by a passer-by, cold and wet, but by then sober! It became a village joke, and Hammercott is said to have claimed the hole for himself by inscribing his name over it.

It is believed the hole was originally a drip well, keeping butter and milk churns cool in bygone years.

Week

The hamlet of Week, with its cluster of thatched cob-walled cottages and Church House, was, in the sixteenth century, the most inhabited part of the parish and for a time boasted a public house – the Champernowne Arms. The Church House, built in 1518, was the first village school, and is said to have been used to accommodate Spanish prisoners from 1866 to 1880. The old family names of Miller, Barnes, Edmonds and Parnell survived here for centuries.

Dart Vale Hunt, originated in 1800 as the Berry Harries, became Dart Vale in 1840. The hunt amalgamated with Haldon after the Second World War and kennelled at Week, Joe Kellock being master and George Heavens huntsman.

For many years the YMCA Youth Hostel was situated in a sixteenth century cottage with low beams, log-burning stove and six bedrooms.

The Old Parsonage/Old Postern

The Old Parsonage, built in the fifteenth century as a parsonage, was altered many times during the following centuries. During 1928/29 major restoration and extension work was carried out under the guidance of Rex Gardner.

James Anthony Froude, the famous historian, was born here in 1818. His father, Robert Hurrell Froude, was Rector of Dartington and Archdeacon of Totnes from 1799 to 1859. From 1891 to 1910 the parsonage was the home of Revd Charles Keble Martin, one of whose sons, William, also became a clergyman and author. The Champernowne family also resided here at various times, and for a short time it was the temporary home of 'LK' and Dorothy Elmhirst when they first arrived in Dartington. In 1928 it was used as a domestic training centre and, during the late 1930s, part of it was run by Toe Ogilvie as a nursery school (which the author attended, although much preferring to feed the ducks!).

In the 1970s the Old Parsonage was part of the sixth-form accommodation of Dartington Hall School and in 1991 became the Schumacher College.

The main entrance to the Parsonage, 1890.

Revd Charles Keble Martin and family, 1893. Left to right, back row: *Arthur, Charlie, Jack, Edith, Katharine, Keble;* middle row: *Nellie, William;* front row: *Revd Charles Martin, Richard, wife Dora.*

Village Scenes

Above: *Dartington Hall lodge in the 1920s and* (below) *in 2003.*

Dartington Hall Lodge

Built in the 1860s at the entrance to the hall estate on the lower drive, the lodge was often surrounded by water when the River Dart flooded. As part of the flood prevention work, a stone wall has since replaced the hedge around the property. Originally the lodge was outside the gates, the stone pillars with iron gates being erected later, with the lodge inside them. In the late 1930s playwright Sean O'Casey lived here while his children were pupils at Dartington Hall School.

Riverford Bridge

In 1805 the Totnes to Buckfastleigh road was opened as a turnpike road, a bridge being built over the River Dart at Hood, on the parish boundary, to bypass the narrow Staverton bridge.

Originally, all bridges in Devon were built and maintained by local builders and quarrymen. In 1808 a new bridge at Fenny Bridges collapsed, and there-after, James Green, a qualified engineer, was appointed to supervise the construction and maintenance of bridges throughout the county.

Staverton Bridge

Though the ford at Staverton was the main crossing point of the Dart for packhorses, until the weir was built at Totnes the river was tidal, thus holding up traffic on the trade route. A narrow wooden construction spanning the river was eventually built, but in 1413 this was replaced with a stone bridge, which is half in Dartington. Measuring 69yds long and only 10ft wide, it has seven obtusely pointed arches, with a bay at the Staverton side which may have held the shrine where tolls were paid. Only wide enough for single traffic, with refuge bays on either side for pedestrians, it is one of Devon's oldest bridges.

It is documented that in 1436 John Laa, curate at Staverton, was attacked on the bridge with a club by parishioner John Gayne and his wife. During the struggle, the curate managed to draw a knife and inflicted a fatal wound on his assailant, who admitted on his deathbed to being the instigator of the struggle. John Laa was acquitted at his trial by Bishop Lacey, on the grounds that he had acted lawfully in self-defence.

Tigley

The railway (originally the South Devon Railway) which skirts the parish boundary from Totnes to Tigley, was opened in May 1848 as broad gauge and converted to standard gauge in 1892. In 1904 the Great Western Railway submitted plans for a new and more level route from Newton Abbot to Brent, via Staverton, Huxham's Cross and Westcombe to Marley Tunnel at Rattery, avoiding the steep Dainton and Rattery gradients.

Staverton Bridge from the Dartington side, 1950 .

The packhorse bridge, Brooking, 2005.

On 13 May 1905, Dartington Parish Council sent a petition to the GWR suggesting that if, or when, a line was constructed through the parish, a station should be built in the neighbourhood of Week. This work, however, was never carried out, due to the cost of such a project.

George Sercombe was a signalman in Tigley box for many years during the 1920s and 1930s.

Brooking

The small hamlet of Brooking, close to Tigley, is situated almost on the parish boundary. There was a girls' school here during the 1870s which closed in 1900, when the headmistress resigned. The children were then transported every day to Dartington school, probably by horse-drawn carriage.

Brooking cottages, 2005.

Dartington limekilns, May 2005.

Dartington textile mill.

✦ CHAPTER 8 ✦

Industries, Farms and Public Houses

Shinner's Bridge Limekilns

The medieval limekilns at Shinner's Bridge were built into an existing bank in the early-nineteenth century. Lime was a very important product in medieval times and such kilns, numerous in south-west Devon in the eighteenth and nineteenth centuries. Fuelled by timber, charcoal or coal, such kilns were used to burn limestone for the production of both lime mortar for building purposes and of lime as an agricultural fertiliser. The two at Dartington were restored in 2003.

Dartington Hall Poultry Department

The Dartington Hall Poultry Department was first established in 1926 by Professor Gustav F. Heuser of Cornell University, with Richard Elmhirst as his assistant. Situated on the north side of Old Parsonage Farm – the first battery-hen farm in Britain, large hen-houses accommodated 2,000 White Leghorns, with other houses for 1,000 chicks.

When Heuser returned to America in 1927, Elmhirst continued to develop the department, adding electricity, an incubator and a battery brooder. The plan was to sell eggs for eating and hatching, but by 1929, with the revenue not enough to make a profit, it was decided to expand and build another unit on fresh land beside the Plymouth road at Yarner, to intensify production.

In 1930 there was a disastrous outbreak of disease caused by *Clostridium butyricum* in poultry food pellets. This resulted in a court case against the company supplying the pellets, a case which, eventually, was lost by Dartington Hall Ltd.

In 1933 there was a change of breed to Light Sussex and Rhode Island Reds, and the hens were allowed to roam and graze on open grassland. Even with a stock of almost 6,000 laying hens, it was still not enough to meet the growing demands.

Richard Elmhirst resigned as manager in 1936, and Miss Mable Whittingham, a professional poultry-woman took over. She introduced a progeny testing scheme to improve the breeding hens, but equipment and hen-houses had to be altered, which proved to be costly in both finance and labour.

When the department was transferred to the Trust in 1940, commercial egg production was stopped and only a stock of breeding birds kept to supply the neighbourhood during the war. The lack of protein in the wartime feed, together with increasing diffi-culty in hiring skilled labour, meant the quality of the hens deteriorated.

In 1942 Mable Whittingham resigned and was succeeded by Miss I.V. Benest, who ran the department until it finally closed in 1945.

Dartington Textile Department

The textile department at Dartington Hall was set up in 1927 by brilliant designer and craftsman Herman (Toby) FitzPatrick, with the help of three assistants. A spinning jack and other machinery was obtained from Wales. Fitzpatrick considered skilled hand-weaving as still superior to machine weaving and his idea was to revive it as a cottage industry, with a small mill for preliminary and finishing processes.

In August 1931 a mill, designed by architect Oswald P. Miln and built by Staverton Builders beside the Bidwell Brook, near Shinner's Bridge, was opened. The plan being to use water power, a large wooden water wheel, transported from a Welsh mill, was installed by local engineers. When the water supply upon which it depended proved at times inadequate, it very soon had to be supplemented by electricity. FitzPatrick's plan for cottage weaving was never achieved, so from the beginning the mill did all the processes, reducing the amount of space within for any other work.

It was almost a year before it came into full production. With four of the staff permanently installing equipment and with limited handlooms, only about half a dozen were engaged in production. However, by the end of 1932 they were achieving a modest output of quality yarns and tweeds. In that

The sluice gate, once used for regulating the water supplied to the mill.

A weaving shed at the textile mill in the 1930s.

Lorraine, Steven and Cathy in the mill's despatch area, November 1987.

year Herr Geisner, from German company I.G. Farbenindustrie, spent several months at the mill teaching the techniques of dyeing.

In 1933 a sheep-breeding experiment, using Welsh Mountain and Shetland Morit breeds on two Dartmoor farms, enabled the mill to test and process their wool for commercial use.

By 1934, FitzPatrick was so involved in research and design that Hiram Winterbotham was appointed production manager. Now consultant and engineer, Fitzpatrick left Dartington shortly afterwards to form his own company. Sadly, in 1936, the charming Irishman took his own life.

Winterbotham overhauled production methods to establish a more secure footing and, as sales increased, he put work out to contract, sending yarn to mills in South Wales. Dartington mill being situated between the Bidwell and steep wooded ground behind, with no room for extension, another small mill in Fordingbridge, Hampshire, was leased, which incurred, because of the distances involved, a great deal of delay and expense.

Winterbotham left in 1939 to become joint managing director of a woollen manufacturers in Stroud. Fred Todkill, his deputy, who had worked in the Yorkshire woollen trade before coming to Dartington in 1932, took over.

In September, when war was declared, rationing of wool made it impossible to maintain high standards, although the introduction of the 'Utility' scheme brought sufficient orders to keep the mill running, with a reduced workforce, throughout the six years of conflict. Plans for a new, larger, mill were

Shinner's Bridge Farm being converted into the cider mill, 1929. (Totnes Image Bank and Rural Archive)

shelved until after the war, but when peace did return, high costs and building restrictions meant it was never built.

Changes were made and by 1951 the department had been reorganised, with Fordingbridge carding and spinning and Dartington weaving and finishing, as well as handling sales and administration. Fred Todkill left in 1954 and Gunnar Storvik, from Norway, took over in 1955, with Welshman Hywel Griffiths as mill manager.

In December 1956, when a fire at the Fordingbridge mill destroyed most of the machinery, the department took over the former grass-drying centre at Lownard Cross, converting it for carding and spinning.

The textile mill closed in November 1987.

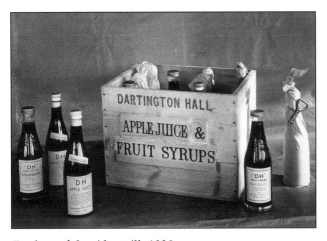

Produce of the cider mill, 1930s.

The Orchards and Cider Making

In 1928 a cider-making mill was created on the site of the old Shinner's Bridge Farm, with surrounding areas developed into apple orchards and fruit plantations. A large Dutch barn was built on the opposite side of the Buckfastleigh road as part of the project. The department was also responsible for growing large quantities of daffodils.

During 1934 a fruit farm was established at Marley Farm, Rattery, where apples, pears, plums, cherries and soft fruits were grown.

In 1935 manager Roger Morel experimented with the making of apple juice at Dartington after visiting factories abroad. Three high-pressure storage tanks, installed in 1936, were the first in Britain, and Dartington cider and apple juice gained a good reputation, winning prizes at agricultural shows.

During the early 1940s the financial situation of the cider mill was causing concern, and in 1944 L. Garvin & Co., of Isleworth, took over the distribution of Dartington cider. By 1947 conditions at Marley Farm proved to be too wet for fruit farming and it was discontinued.

The cider mill closed in 1952 and the company was liquidated in 1957.

Dartington Sawmill

In 1929 it was decided that the small sawmill at the hall was inadequate to deal with the new plans for forestry around the estate, and a more spacious

Lunch break at the cider mill, 1935. From left: *Anthony Morel, Roger Morel, ?, ?, Cecil Barrett, Ernest Miller.* standing: *John Sercombe.*

A steam wagon at the entrance to the sawmill, early 1930s.

The Duke of Kent arriving at the sawmill, accompanied by the Elmhirsts.

site, on the Plymouth Road near Shinner's Bridge, was selected .

Built by Staverton Builders and opened in 1932, the new sawmill was built along American lines under the management of George Turner, who had previously been to America to study layout and equipment for the project. Until the new Dartington plantations reached maturity, projected to be in about 50 years, there was enough timber within a transport radius of approximately 70 miles to feed the mill. A disadvantage was its distance from the railway. If the mill had had its own sidings, there would have been big savings in production costs. With most round timber arriving by road, the majority of sawn timber was dispatched by rail and, prior to the war, double-handling cost an extra halfpenny per cubic foot on every order. After 1950, most of the sawn timber was also delivered by road.

The mill was electrically powered, while two large boilers, brought from a disused Cornish tin mine and fuelled by sawdust and waste timber, produced steam for heating and for the generating plant. Timber arriving at the sawmill was stacked under the gantry, cut to specifications, then moved into the main shop for sawing, before being stacked ready for dispatch to customers in London, the Midlands or Wales. In the early days transport was by horses and steam lorries, but this soon changed to petrol and diesel vehicles. Although there were plenty of orders – planking for railway wagons, pit props for mines and furniture squares – it took several years before profits were made.

The Forestry Department was separated into two – Woodlands, which operated under the Dartington Hall Trust and Sawmills, under Dartington Hall Ltd.

From 1937 P.H. Taylor was manager until called up for war service in 1940. Ernest G. Clake replaced him as department manager, with K. Hobbs as mill manager. The war years brought many large orders from the Ministry of Supply and women were employed to replace the men called up into the Armed Forces. For a time after Dunkirk, with the threat of invasion, the mill operated seven days a

week, supplying timber for urgent defence work around the South Coast.

In 1940 the Duke of Kent, who was serving in the RAF, visited the mill as a guest of the Elmhirsts. He was killed on 25 August 1942, when the Sunderland Flying Boat he was in crashed onto a Scottish mountain while flying to Iceland.

By 1942 staff were working 60 hours a week, and during the war years over a million cubic feet of timber was processed, yielding 775,000 cubic feet of sawn timber. Wood was being supplied to Totnes shipyard for building minesweepers and, later, landing craft, and to the Ministry of Supply, to British and American forces, to coal mines and to railways.

After the war, in 1946 a new woodworking department took over the making of furniture from the carpentry and turnery shops, producing garden furniture. Unable to compete with larger companies, however, the department closed in 1952. A recession in the timber trade resulted in the carpentry and turnery work being taken back from the wood-working department.

In 1959, Dartington Hall Trust went into partnership with F.J. Reeves & Co. (Totnes) to form Dartington Sawmills Ltd, but went into voluntary liquidation in 1981. The site is, at the time of writing, Webber's Yard Industrial Estate.

Dartington Woodlands Department

Prior to the Elmhirsts arriving at Dartington Hall, forestry had become neglected. That was to change when Tom Brown arrived to take charge. The research urgently needed in the techniques of growing trees and in forest economics was not available to private landowners under government funding. For new forest plantations, it was necessary

Woodlands Department workers c.1950. Left to right, back row: *William 'Jack' James, Joe Heath, Len and Tom Webber, ?;* front row: *Jim Pounsland, Douglas Lambert, Robert Penn, Jim Miller;* kneeling: *Arthur Harris.*

The north woods c.1950, with Tom Webber on the lorry and Len Webber loading.

to clear 50 acres a year of scrub, which meant large financial costs, with estimates of 20–30 years before new plantations became commercially profitable and 45–50 years before a forest was established.

In May 1928 the 332-acre Kingswood, near Buckfastleigh, was bought, and in October, 1,200 acres of Hambleden Estate, near Moretonhampstead, were purchased. The forestry department disbanded in April 1932, its work being divided between the

Sawmills Department and the Woodlands Department, the latter operating directly under the Trust and in charge of all plantations and the cultivation of trees . The department was directed by Wilfred E. Hiley, previously a member of Oxford School of Forestry, while Tom Brown continued as forester in charge of the woods.

The department had two sawmills, one at Dartington and the other at Moretonhampstead, due to the location of the woods. When war broke out the department was thrust into profit making because of the urgent need for timber at higher prices. Felling had to be more severe than was anticipated, with the demand for poles and pickets for South-east coastal defences, pit props for coal mines and oak for railway sleepers. Most of the oak coppices were replanted with conifer trees, which increased the values.

In January 1949 the department became Dartington Woodlands Ltd. In 1956 Wilfred Hiley, a director from 1946 to 1958, was awarded the CBE. In 1965 the Department was awarded the Royal Forestry Society Gold Medal and in 1966 the Forestry Training Centre was set up.

Dartington Pottery

Bernard Leach, who had started a pottery at St Ives, Cornwall, in 1920, came to Dartington in 1927 to practise his skills in a small studio at the hall. In

Dartington Pottery, 1980s.

1933, when a large pottery workshop was built near the disused quarry at Shinner's Bridge, Leach's son, David, arrived and the pottery began to produce in a steady way. David left the following year to do technical training and in 1937 Leach built, close by, a small wooden house, 'The Cabin', where he wrote *A Potter's Book*, published in 1940. When he returned to St Ives in 1941, the pottery stood empty.

Marianne de Trey, born in London in 1913 of Swiss parents, married Sam Haile, a potter and painter, in 1938, and the following year they moved to America, where she worked as a textile designer before starting to make pottery. In 1943 her husband enlisted in the US Army, then transferred to the British Army and was posted to England. Marianne followed in 1945 and, after his demob, they both worked in Suffolk as full-time potters.

In 1947 they arrived in Dartington to take over the derelict pottery at Shinner's Bridge, living in 'The Cabin', where Leach had lived. Together they renovated the pottery and built two new kilns. Sam also worked as a part-time adviser to small potteries, which involved a lot of travelling. It was on one of his trips in March of the following year that he was killed in a car accident in Dorset. Their daughter, Sarah, was born shortly afterwards, and with the help of her sisters, Judy and Ann, who looked after the baby, Marianne continued potting. Production increased and by the 1950s she had five employees.

In March 1957 a serious fire, caused by faulty wiring on the electric kiln, destroyed the pottery. Marianne rebuilt the business, installing an oil-fired kiln which was later replaced with a wood-fired one, and for over 40 years ran a very successful pottery workshop, producing domestic wares and training a number of apprentices. Her work was often exhibited both in Britain and abroad.

Marianne retired in 1982, moving to a small studio nearby to carry on her pottery skills at leisure. Dartington Pottery Training Workshop took over the premises, which closed in 2005.

At the age of 92, Marianne de Trey was awarded the CBE in the 2006 New Year's Honours list.

Barton Farm

Situated inside the north end of the hall courtyard, Barton Farm, under the Champernownes, was a mixed farm of dairy and beef cattle, with sheep, pigs and poultry. It was owned by the Codd family, which consisted of unmarried brothers and their aunt, with Frank Crook as manager.

When the Elmhirsts purchased Dartington Hall in 1925, plans were made for the farm to be moved across the road, to enable the courtyard and surrounding buildings to be redeveloped. The Codds finally left in 1928 and that same year new farm buildings, stables and a Dutch barn were built. Fred Crook continued as manager, and in 1930 work started on farm workers' cottages.

During the war years a good deal of grazing ground was ploughed up so that extra crops, including potatoes, wheat and sugar beet, could be grown to help feed the nation. In 1952, when a milking parlour and semi-covered collecting yard for 80 cows were built, Ayrshire cattle replaced the existing South Devons.

Old Parsonage Farm

In 1926 Old Parsonage Farm was purchased from the rector by Leonard Elmhirst, who appointed C.F. Nielsen, a Dane who spoke very good English, as manager. His plan was to create an intensive dairy farm, and he removed over two miles of hedges and banks, making one field alone – which became known as 'Sneezles's Prairie' – over 70 acres. In 1931 he designed new buildings which gave all-weather protection to farm workers and animals. He also introduced milking machines and equipment for cooling and bottling milk. All floors were concrete with facilities for washing them down, a wide gutter taking liquid manure into a large underground tank. Five horses supplied the power before the first tractor arrived, and the farm was run by a staff of 16. In 1932 the farmhouse and workers' cottages were completed. Nielsen concentrated on the improve-

Sam Kerswell with a South Devon cow in the 1950s.

Farm workers' children, early 1950s. From left: Anthony and Terry Kerswell, ?, Alan Brown.

ment of the South Devon breed of cattle for their milk and butter, and by 1933 a herd of 60 was milking three times a day.

The two farms had a good reputation for their cattle during the 1930s and won many prizes at the London Dairy and other agricultural shows. Nielsen finally left in December 1937 to start his own farm (he died in 1965). Frank Crook took over as joint manager of both farms until he gave up farming in 1945 and retired. The new manager was Ronald Hawtin, who had worked on the farm in the 1930s, and who later became manager of a farm in Cornwall. In 1954 the South Devon herd was gradually reduced and replaced by Friesians, the last South Devon being sold in 1962.

In 1974 Francis Huntington was appointed director of Dartington Hall Farms Ltd.

Foxhole School Farm

The school farm, started in 1932, was an idea of headmaster W.B. Curry, and allowed the children of the nearby school to work, if they wished, on the 60-acre farm during school terms. It enabled them to learn about farming, not only in the classroom, but to actu-

Bringing in the hay at Foxhole in the 1940s.

ally take part, learning about animals, tools, machinery and crops, much of the farm produce being used in the school kitchen. A mixture of Guernsey, Kerry and South Devon cattle, two horses called Punch and Judy, pigs, poultry and a herd of goats made up the livestock.

Public Houses

Ye Old Cott Inne

The Cott Inn, originally two cottages, was converted in 1320 by Johannes Cott, a wealthy merchant, into a staging-post for drovers and their packhorses. Claimed to be the second oldest public house in England, it has cob walls over 2ft thick and its thatched roof measures 194ft long. The decline of the wool and tin trades meant the end of packhorses, and the pub became a small village alehouse, with a few regulars as customers. Over the years many old Dartington family names – Searle, Parnell and Barnes – were linked with the pub. During the late 1930s and early 1940s, Percy Parnell looked after three cows and some pigs housed in adjoining buildings, his two fields being where Newman Crescent and Tolchers housing estate are now built (2007). Trade flourished in 1943 and early 1944, when American

Believed to be the Cott Inne pump, 1830. The lady is unknown.

105

Ye Old Cott Inne, 1930. (Totnes Image Bank and Rural Archive)

Firemen damping down, August 1989.

The pub interior, c.1950.

The Queen's Arms.

The Dart Vale Hunt sets off from the Cott Inn, Boxing Day, 1953.

troops crowded into the small bar to mix with the locals, who often coaxed them to sample a pint of Devon 'scrumpy' cider!

In 1947 Sam Mearing, from Kent, purchased the premises, together with the adjoining cottage, cattle buildings and hayloft, which were converted into a lounge bar, dining-room, kitchen and guest bedrooms. The pigsty was demolished, the gardens became a large car park, the roof was re-thatched and the exterior painted white. Since that time there have been several licensees and the inn has become known worldwide, numbering among its guests many foreigners, celebrities and politicians.

In August 1989 a fire caused £100,000 worth of damage to the fourteenth-century pub. With flames ripping through the roof and bedrooms, 13 guests were led to safety. Firemen managed to save part of the thatched roof after tackling the blaze for several hours, the thatch being over 4ft thick in places. It took many months to restore the burnt roof beams and to re-thatch the roof – 17 tons of Austrian water-reed were used – but the inn carried on trading throughout the renovations.

The Queen's Arms
The Queen's Arms is situated on the A385 as you enter the village from Totnes. It was originally used for the drying and bailing of wool before it was loaded onto barges, which came up the tidal estuary, now known as Bidwell meadow. The pub is said to have been named after Queen Elizabeth I, who reputedly landed there on a visit to the Champernownes at Dartington Hall. It was converted into a public house some time after 1585, when the estuary ceased to be.

♦ CHAPTER 9 ♦

Clubs and Scouts

Dartington and District Motorcycle Club

When the Second World War ended and servicemen from the parish returned home, several of them purchased motorcycles – cars being a luxury in those days! Cott Cross became a meeting-place on a Sunday morning, my father doing minor repairs/adjustments on their bikes. Later he rented a large wooden shed adjacent to the Cott Inn, and used it as a workshop for several years during evenings and weekends. Eventually he and John Sercombe, along with other enthusiasts, formed a motorcycle club, with a chairman, secretary, treasurer and club captain, some members coming to join from as far afield as Totnes and Buckfastleigh.

Organised runs on a Sunday afternoon became a regular event, with wives, sisters and girlfriends on the pillion seats. Sometimes four or five bikers participated, at other times a dozen or more, but these trips were always enjoyed, whatever the numbers. Riders would rendezvous at Cott Cross, then set off across Dartmoor, or along the south Devon coast or take the Saltash Ferry across the Tamar and venture into Cornwall.

Edgar Hodge, club treasurer.

George 'Jeff' MacLening, Cott Cross, 1958.

Right: *At Haytor, 1947. From left: Albert Tucker, Claire, Jeff and Mike MacLening.*

Left: *At Haytor Rock, Dartmoor, 1946. From left: Keith Gill, John Sercombe and Jeff MacLening.*

Left: *Taking a break when crossing Dartmoor. From left: Eric Clark, Keith Gill, Dick Legg, Betty Sercombe, Avis Clements, Beryl Gill; in front: Jeff MacLening.*

Right: *A roadside stop in Cornwall, 1949. Left to right, back row: John Sercombe, Ted King, Dennis Fricker, Mike and Jeff MacLening; front row: Betty Sercombe, Albert Tucker, Barbara King.*

Left: *Hold on tight, Betty! John Sercombe and his sister in a motorcycle scramble, Yelverton, 1949.*

Right: *Edward 'Ted' King in the late 1940s.*

On Dartmoor, 1949. Left to right, back row: *John and Betty Sercombe, Frank and Maud Brown, Douglas Marshall; front: Dick Legg, ?, Claire MacLening.*

Left: *John Sercombe on his AJS trials bike, 1949.*

Right: *At Slapton Sands in the mid-1950s. From left to right: ?, Jeff MacLening, Betty Sercombe, Barbara King; sitting: Ted King, John Sercombe.*

A few members, notably John Sercombe and Edward 'Ted' King, participated in several local motorcycle scramble trials.

When petrol rationing was reintroduced, the club disbanded and never reformed although, when fuel rationing was abolished, a few original members carried on the Sunday runs into the '50s and '60s, before two wheels gave way to four wheels – the family car had arrived!

Dartington Youth Club

During the late 1940s and early '50s the Youth Club, for those aged 13–17 years, was held on Monday evenings at 7.30–9.30p.m. in the Central Offices.

Youth Club badge from the 1940s–1950s.

Gone Dutch! Dartington members on a youth club visit to Holland in 1952. From left: Rosemary Tuffnell, Julia Morgan, Pamela Parnell.

Several years later, a decline in membership led to the club's closure. In 1963 a new youth club was opened, and in 1969 the Dartington Youth Club opened at Meadowbrook, with Wesley Jones as leader.

The 1st Dartington Scout Troop

The Scout movement was formed in 1908 by Lord Robert 'B.P.' Baden-Powell who, in August 1929, was made a baron for his work in the Scout movement worldwide. It is not known when scouting first began in the parish, but in the early 1930s Horace Davis was scoutmaster of Dartington Troop.

In the Scouting calendar, the highlight of the year was the annual summer camp, a favourite camping ground with local troops being for many years beside the River Dart at Hood, beneath Hood Ball.

Scoutmaster Horace Davis, 1934, probably while camping at Hood.

Douglas Denham (left) *and Len Hodge.*

The author, May 1947.

Eggesford, North Devon, August 1948. Standing from left: *Mike MacLening and David 'Chips' Rafferty;* sitting from left: *Michael Coombes and Fred Widger.*

When I joined the 1st Dartington Troop, in April 1945, there were about a dozen members, consisting of a Curlew and an Owl patrol. Keith Gill was scout-master with Horace Fice his assistant. Headquarters, in woods close to the textile mill, consisted of a small timber hut with no windows, which became rather crowded during the Thursday evening meetings.

In 1946 Robert 'Bob' Penn, with years of Scouting experience, moved to the village to work for the Woodlands Department and took over as Scoutmaster, moving the HQ to a larger stone-built building at Shinner's Bridge – originally the Home Guard HQ – which was more convenient. Bob remained Scoutmaster for many years and was a first class 'Skipper'.

Camping was an event all the boys looked forward to. The 'trek' cart, loaded with tents, cooking utensils, tools, blankets, kit-bags with personal effects, water containers and food, would be pushed and pulled (with a rope) along the road, which was quieter in those days, to the occasional toot from a passing vehicle! We stopped for a breather about every hour.

On arrival at a suitable site, usually close to a stream or river and woods, tents were erected and a latrine pit, with screens around, dug a considerable distance from camp. Fire-wood was collected and a fire lit ready for a welcome 'brew', while drinking water and milk (sometimes eggs) were obtained from the nearest farm.

Reveille was at seven o'clock, and after breakfast there were chores to do. Tent sides were hung up, blankets aired, milk, water and firewood collected and dinner prepared. Scouting activities included semaphore signalling, making knots, fire-lighting with dry leaves and twigs and hiking. Evenings were spent around the log camp-fire having a sing-song or, while 'Skip' told a ghost story, nervously peering over our shoulders into the darkness if a rabbit scuttled close by or an owl suddenly hooted!

In April 1946 I was promoted to patrol leader and, in April 1949, was awarded a four-year 'star'. At the end of January 1950, because of my shift-work on the railway, I reluctantly left the troop, having enjoyed almost five years of Scouting.

Robert Penn died on 16 September 1996, aged 82, and is buried in Dartington cemetery.

Scout Camps

28 July–4 August 1945	*Shipley Bridge, Didworthy*
23–26 May 1947	*Hood Ball*
2–10 August 1947	*Harford Moor, Ivybridge*
15–7 May 1948	*Hood Ball*
31 July–7 August 1948 (by rail)	*Eggesford, N. Devon*
4–6 June 1949	*Jamboree at Dawlish*

People of the Parish

Mrs Polly Barnes and family, Puddaven Cottage, in the 1890s. Seated left *is Polly Young.*

Above left: *Polly Barnes* (centre) *and family members, c.1900. Above right: Polly Barnes in the 1890s.*

❖ CHAPTER 10 ❖

People of the Parish

David James, from Village to Heritage

David James, a Dartington boy, attended the village Primary School and Redworth Secondary School, Totnes, leaving at the age of 14. He then joined Staverton Builders as an apprentice carpenter and joiner, followed by two years' National Service in the RAF.

During his working life David was a civilian instructor with REME and a contract carpenter; he spent five years with SWEB (the South West Electricity Board) and 22 years as a clerk of works at King's College, Taunton.

David James, c.1950.

David outside his Postbox Museum, 2006.

Retiring in 1990, he set up his own private collection of letterboxes, dating from Victorian times to the present day, a hobby which has taken him all over the country, collecting and restoring the boxes, most of them in very bad condition and with parts missing. He has restored a Hong Kong King George V postbox, of which there are only two in existence, the other being in the Hong Kong Postal Museum. Other memorabilia have included stamp machines, telephone kiosks, clocks, sewing machines, old signs – you name it, David probably collects it!

At the Inkpen Postbox Museum at Thurlbear, near Taunton, this unique private collection, part of our heritage, demonstrates one man's dedication, and that of his wife, Kate, to a fascinating hobby.

Ivy Parnell

Aged 95 at the time of writing, Ivy Parnell (née Edmonds), one of Dartington's oldest residents, was born in the village and has lived here all her life. She met her future husband, Victor, who came from Harberton, at a dance in the local Village Hall. They were married in 1933 and had two children, Pamela and Anthony.

Ivy worked at the Old Postern in the days when it was a school, and in later years was treasurer of Dartington Senior Club. Victor worked in the Dartington Hall gardens, was a keen fisherman and for many years was a bell-ringer at the local church

Ivy Parnell, 2005.

People of the Parish

Mr and Mrs N. Heath and daughter, Ella, and son, Alfred, Steps Cottage, Staple, 1890. Ella died in 1965, aged 91, Alfred in 1908, aged only 34.

Sarah 'Nellie' Almond, c.1900.

James Henry Almond in the 1930s.

People of the Parish

Wear a hat and get ahead! Village lads in the 1920s. From left: *Eddie Guy, Edgar Hodge, Lester and Douglas Denham, Edgar Holwell.*

From left: *Ivy Barnes, Claude Barnes, Louie Barnes, Percy Barnes. Cott Road, 1925.*

Left: *Ellen Barnes, Forge Cottage, Cott Road, 1920.*

and at Totnes and Buckfast Abbey. During the war he served in the Royal Navy.

They celebrated their golden wedding anniversary in 1983. Victor died in October 1988 and Ivy is now a resident at Forder House.

Pam Gorman

Born in Wrangaton, Pamela Gorman's early years were spent at boarding school at Avonwick. In the late 1940s her family moved to Dartington, where she attended Redworth Secondary School, Totnes.

From an early age Pam was interested in drawing and art and, on leaving school she went on to attend St Luke's College, Exeter, taking art as her main subject. She later taught art to primary schoolchildren for seven years.

Eventually she gave up teaching to work for VSO (Voluntary Service Overseas), spending 3¹/₂ years in Montserrat, in the West Indies, living in a mountain hut among the villagers. As well as teaching them art and crafts, Pam also taught the adults to read and write. While there, Pam learned leatherworking from a local shoemaker.

Returning to Britain, Pam set up a business making leather jewellery, becoming a member of the ADL (the Association of Designer Leatherworkers), which organised leatherwork exhibitions in England. She has travelled throughout Canada, America and South Africa, working on art-related projects.

Pam uses acrylics, oils and pen and ink in her pictures, which have been exhibited a number of times, winning various prizes. Her favourites among her paintings are those of Yarner Beacon, a landmark which can be seen from her house.

Now retired, in 2007 Pam still continues painting in her studio, and also enjoys gardening, walking, reading and African drumming!

Cecile Milton, MBE

Former Dartington resident Cecile Milton (née MacLening) was invested with the MBE by the Queen at Buckingham Palace on 10 March 1998.

The award was made in recognition of her work on behalf of the postal service and local community in the Sussex village where she lived for many years.

Cecile was a pupil at Dartington Primary School,

Pamela Gorman, in August 1974, at the Birdwood House Exhibition with one of her many paintings of Yarner Beacon.

Yarner Beacon, by Pamela Gorman.

Cecile Milton and husband, John, outside Buckingham Palace with her MBE.

People of the Parish

Bertha Holwell with her daughters, Ruth and Loveda, c. 1920.

Ernest and Harriet Miller at Week in the 1930s.

Ruth Holwell in the 1930s.

Bertha Holwell with daughter Loveday in the 1930s.

People of the Parish

Tom Gribble.

Bertha Holwell and Elizabeth Gribble at Staple.

Edgar Holwell.

Violet Dommett and Pat Winson in the late 1930s.

Old Church House, Week, the Passmore family home, with Annie Passmore in the doorway.

William 'Bill' Passmore in the 1920s.

then at the former Girls' County School, Totnes, residing first at Newman Crescent and later at Parsonage Cottages.

John, her husband, was herdsman at Old Parsonage Farm, then, in the late 1940s and early '50s at Barton Farm .

William Passmore

In September 1954 78-year-old William Passmore, who lived at Week and had been totally blind for 14 years, knocked his head in the shed while shovelling coal. The next morning he woke up, looked around

People of the Parish

George MacLening, Dartington Hall lower drive, 1933.

Claire MacLening, 1933.

Violet Newson with son Tony in his pram, Puddaven, October 1933.

Ernest and Francis Miller in the 1930s.

Harold and Lilly Hodge, 1943.

Right: *Roy* (left) *and Gwen Edwards and friend in the 1940s.*

People of the Parish

Reg Newson with his GWR lorry, 1944. Note the masked headlamp – a wartime restriction.

Barry Nash, 1944.

Jessie Matthews in the 1940s.

Staff from the workers' canteen at the Social Centre, Shinner's Bridge, c.1948. From the left: ?, Josie Popplestone, Ciss MacLening, ?, Mrs Dance, Claire MacLening. The young boy is Andrew MacLening.

Cecile, Ciss (back), Nigel and Audrey MacLening, Newman Crescent, 1949. Nigel and Audrey now live in W. Australia.

Julia Morgan and Rosemary Tuffnell at Redlake in the late 1940s.

People of the Parish

Village girls, c.1949. Left to right, back row: *Winnie Buckingham, Mary Philpot, Pat Winson, Beryl Gill, Nancy Prout, Gwen James;* middle row: *Ellen Tuffnell, Barbara Everett, Betty Sercombe, Violet Dommett;* front row: *Pat Hill, Daphne Martin, Violet Arscott.*

Lazing in the sun in the late 1940s. The photo includes Bill Brooks, Pat Wilson, Nancy Prout and Betty Sercombe.

People of the Parish

Violet Newson and son Tony, with Dorothy Morgan (centre) at Dartington Hall in the late 1940s.

June Hocking, Betty James and Julia Morgan at Crossing Cross, c.1950.

Harold and Lilly Hodge in their Ford, c.1950.

Members of the Dart Rowing Club, c.1950. Left to right, back row: Betty Sutherland, Pat Winson, Nancy Prout; front row: Joan Veale, Betty Lindop.

Pat Winson at Crossways, c.1950.

All aboard! Parsonage Farm workers' outing, 1928. The photo includes William Passmore (standing, second from left).

People of the Parish

Dorothy Morgan with daughter Julia and Betty Sercombe at a church wedding, c.1950.

Pamela Parnell and Rosemary Tuffnell, early 1950s.

Hilda Gill and daughter Beryl, early 1950s.

Valerie Lake and Julia Morgan in the 1950s.

Audrey MacLening and Rosemary Tuffnell, 3 June 1951.

People of the Parish

Betty James, Julia Morgan and June Walters, c.1955.

Steven Hodge with Tracey and Audrey Neville, Redlake, c.1960.

John Sercombe (left) and Jeff MacLening in the garden machinery repair workshop, Webber's Yard industrial estate (previously the saw mills), May 1973.

Janet (left) and Carol James at Redlake, 1967.

Bill Passmore with his grandchildren, September 1954.

and suddenly realised he could see again!

Poor sight had troubled William from an early age, but when he joined the 5th Devonshire Regiment in the First World War, poor scores on the rifle range resulted in him being diagnosed with eye problems. Despite hospital treatment his sight got worse and he was taken off military duties to do farm work until his discharge from the Army. Returning to civilian life in the village, he carried on with farm work and gardening until, in 1940, the complete loss of his remaining sight compelled him to give up work.

It was 14 years later that Bill made local and national newspaper headlines, his greatest joy being that he could see his grandchildren for the first time!

Annie, his wife, died only a few months later, on 11 November 1954, aged 82, and Bill the following year, on 29 June 1955, aged 79.

Characters from Dartington's Past

Peter Clear

Peter Clear, born in 1756, was a jobbing carpenter who made and repaired carts and other agricultural implements, as well as selling timber and firewood. His workshop was at Threecorners House, Longcause. He worked on the Champernowne estates and was involved in work on the Surrey Light Dragoon Barracks in 1794. He would hire out as a carrier, travelling with his horse and cart as far as Plymouth, Exeter and Ottery St Mary. He married Mary Baker in 1778 and made his last Will in January 1842, by which time he was blind. He left his property to his daughter, Joanne (a widow), to sons Peter and John and to Joanne's daughter, Ann. He died in 1846 aged 90.

'Poll' Harries

Mrs 'Poll' Harries cleaned Dartington Hall Church in the early part of the nineteenth century. It was said that, after she cleaned the floor, you could eat your food off it! She worked for the Hannaford family at Bellany Farm, near Week, and did their washing every Monday of her own accord. On one occasion she entered Gidley Hannaford in the local baby show, where he won a silver cup.

Charlotte Champernowne

Miss Charlotte Elizabeth Champernowne, who died on 1 April 1968 at the age of 93, was the eldest daughter and last surviving child of Arthur Champernowne and his wife, Helen Melville. She took a lively interest in family affairs right up to her death, and kept in touch with events at Dartington. Although the loss of the old family home had been a cause of great grief to her, she had long come to realise that it was in loving hands with the Elmhirsts. Although 'Bessie' Champernowne's generation had come to an end, in her time there had been ten members of the family at Dartington Hall, with nine cousins at the Old Parsonage.

Charlie Llewellyn

Charlie Llewellyn was born on 3 July 1898 in Abergavenny, South Wales, one of eight children (he had one brother and six sisters). His father was a miner, his mother a farmer's daughter. Leaving school at 14, he also became a miner, at Vartic Colliery. In 1918, aged 20, he was called up to serve in the First World War. Demobbed in 1919, he bought his first horse and returned to the mines until 1926, when he came to Devon.

He first worked at the Symonds Cider Factory on The Plains in Totnes, then on the Dartington estate. When the Second World War broke out, he joined the RAF, serving at Harrowbeer, Yelverton, then for four years at Rissington, Yorkshire. After the war, he returned to work on the Dartington estate until he retired at the age of 65. Charlie then worked as a groundsman at the Primary School until he was 80. He lived at Staple, where he kept chickens and horses, breaking in his last horse, Biscuit, at the age of 88. Charlie celebrated his 100th birthday in 1998 and died two years later, in his 102nd year.

Thomas Bramwell Bartlett

'Bram' – as he was known throughout his life – arrived in the village from Newton Abbot in about 1946, the family moving into a house in Broad View, opposite the Cott Inn.

He and his elder brother, John, soon teamed up with the local lads, taking part in the usual pranks (no details!), cycle rides and football matches against Foxhole School on a Sunday afternoon – Bram, being over 6ft tall, made the ideal centre half. Leaving Redworth Secondary School in 1949, he joined Staverton Builders as an apprentice carpenter and joiner, working in Buckfast Abbey and County Hall, Exeter. Then followed two years' National Service in the RAF Regiment.

A keen sportsman, Bram played football for Dartington United and Harberton. He also played squash and tennis, being a Lawn Tennis Association coach, and was very useful as both batsman and bowler when playing cricket for the College of Arts.

He joined the college as a carpenter in 1963 and in September 1968 married his wife, Mary, in the village church – Bram made much of the furniture for their house. They had two daughters, Lucy and Emma. In 1992 Bram became the estate warden and, with his knowledge of natural history and wildlife, for eight years he wrote the 'Bram's Patch' article in the estate newsletter about its wildlife.

Retiring from full-time employment in 1999 after 50 years' service, Bram continued working as a part-

time warden, guiding walks around the estate for local schools and for history groups. In 2003 Bram was diagnosed with mesothelioma, a cancer brought on by his contact with asbestos during his working life. He battled against the illness for two years until his death in September 2005, aged 71. The church was packed at his funeral – a final tribute to 'Bram'.

Duggie Hart

Douglas Hart, a skilled woodturner, was a kind and friendly character, well known throughout the village for many years. Born in London in 1919, he came to Dartington at an early age in the 1920s. A pupil at Dartington Hall School, he then did a wood-

'Bram' Bartlett, c.1980.

Duggie Hart at work.

turning apprenticeship, setting up his own workshop in the 1950s and training many of Britain's wood craftsmen. Visitors to the village could watch Duggie at work, producing bowls, plates, spinning tops and a variety of children's toys. Any donations for this privilege were given to charity. Duggie also produced work for the royal household and for many top London stores. For many years he lived at 'Aiblins', Cott Lane, before moving to Brimhay. He died at the age of 77.

Duggie Hart's workshop at the Cider Press Centre.

CHAPTER 11

Winter Around the Village

Jimmy Stubbins (front) *and Tony Newson, January 1945. The field overlooking Shinner's Bridge was a favourite sledging ground for children (and adults) in bygone years.*

Flooded fields either side of Dartington Hall lower drive in the 1950s.

The Cott Inn from Cott Lane, January 1963. (Totnes Image Bank and Rural Archive)

Entrance to the Cott Inn, January 1963. (Totnes Image Bank and Rural Archive)

Arctic scenery! Snow and icicles cover the water-wheel, January 1963.

The lodge gates, Dartington Hall lower drive, January 1963.

The lodge.

Dartington Hall gardens.

Cott Cross Cottage, January 1964.

The summerhouse in winter!

The Cott Inn, c.1970.

The Social Centre, c.1980. Built in 1930, in 2007 it is the Tridias Toyshop.

This could be Switzerland, but it's Marianne de Trey and Peter Cook outside The Cabin and Pottery, Shinner's Bridge, in the late 1980s.

A snow-plough clearing Cott Road in the 1990s.

Cott Road looking towards Shinner's Bridge, c.1990.   *Redlake Cross Bridge, 1999.*

Bidwell Brook in Flood

On Wednesday, 7 February 1990, torrential rain caused the usually gently flowing Bidwell Brook to burst its banks in the centre of the village, flooding the Primary School playground and rising beneath temporary classrooms. As a precaution, the pupils were sent home and told to stay away the following day while any damage was assessed. The water did not enter any of the buildings and the children were allowed to return two days later.

The grounds of the Cider Press Centre were also flooded as the water reached the top of the stone bridge archway.

Flood water flows into the Primary School playground, 7 February 1990.

CHAPTER 12

Sports

Dartington Hall workers compete in a tug-of-war in the 1920s. (Totnes Image Bank and Rural Archive)

The Village Football Clubs

For many years, both before and after the Second World War, Dartington United FC played in the South Devon League (Senior Division), playing their home matches on the Foxhole sports field. In the early 1950s they moved to a new ground, adjacent to the first, which was formerly an orchard.

Several of the long-serving players, notably Ken Boon, Len Kerslake and Frank Lake, donned their 'whites' during the summer months to play for the village cricket XI. Veteran Frank Lake became a football referee (Class 1) after finally hanging up his boots in the early '50s.

On Saturday, 8 February 1930, Dartington United were playing at Kingsteignton when, after no more than 10 minutes, the ball burst and the referee abandoned the game!

During the early 1960s, another village team, Meadowbrook Football Club, was founded. Originally formed from youth club members, the team played their home matches on the Dorothy Elmhirst playing-field.

Dartington United and Totnes, rivals for years, have now amalgamated and, at the time of writing, participate in the Axworthys' Devon League.

Dartington Football Club badge.

Dartington United FC
South Devon League, Senior Division

1954-55 (30 matches)

	w	d	l	pts
Ipplepen Athletic	22	4	4	48
Dartmouth Y.M.	21	4	5	46
Moreton	19	3	8	41
Upton Athletic	18	4	8	40
Ashburton	18	4	8	40
Bovey	17	4	9	38
Dartside Rovers	16	4	10	36
Kingsteignton Ath. Res.	16	2	12	34
Stoke Gabriel	12	3	15	27
St. M'church Spurs Res.	12	2	16	26
Brixham Villa	11	3	16	25
Collaton United.	8	5	17	21
Hele Spurs Res.	6	6	18	18
Paignton Town Res.	5	4	21	14
Bishopsteignton United	5	3	22	13
Dartington United	3	6	21	12

1955-56 (30 matches)

	w	d	l	goals for	against	pts
Hele Spurs Res.	26	2	2	118	35	54
6th Boys Trng. Regt.	24	1	5	138	55	49
Ashburton	19	2	9	86	69	40
Bovey	17	4	9	120	77	38
K'steignton Ath Res.	16	3	11	119	69	35
Beesands Res.	14	7	9	67	51	35
Totnes United	15	0	15	91	94	30
St. M'church Spurs Res.	11	7	12	70	64	29
Brixham Villa	13	2	15	66	77	28
Moreton	9	9	12	80	88	27
Dartington United	11	2	17	67	99	24
Bishopsteignton United	9	5	16	56	78	23
Stoke Gabriel	7	9	14	70	83	23
Dartside Rovers	8	5	17	72	104	21
Collaton United	8	2	20	78	140	18
Paignton Town Res.	0	6	24	33	149	6

1956-57 (26 matches)

	w	d	l	pts
Kingsteignton Ath. Res.	25	0	1	50
Stoke Gabriel	22	2	2	46
Bovey	18	3	5	39
Brixham Villa	16	4	6	36
Dartmouth Y.M.	14	4	8	32
Kingsbridge Athletic	11	3	12	25
Dartington United	9	4	13	22
St. M'church Spurs Res.	9	3	14	21
Ashburton	10	1	15	21
Hele Spurs Res.	7	6	13	20
Paignton Town Res.	9	1	16	19
Moreton	5	5	16	15
Totnes United	6	1	19	13
Dartside Rovers	1	3	22	5

Dartington Hall Football Club, 1933/34. Left to right, back row: *Les Markham, Jack Last, Cecil Gidley, Frank Lake, Len Kerslake, Tommy Hardman, Jack Gallon;* middle row: *Tommy Nicholson, Bert Philips, Frank Lane;* front row: *Ernie Bone, Toby Finch, Tommy Gardiner, 'Cast' Kinsman, Ernie Jacobs.* (Totnes Image Bank and Rural Archive)

Dartington United in the 1950s. Left to right, back row: *? Taylor, Dave Phillips, ?, Edgar Miller, Jimmy Mills, ?, Ken Winchester, ? Clark;* front row: *Edgar Hodge, ?, Fred Redshaw, Derek Clark, Eddie Dolley.*

Events and Celebrations

A Dartington Hall workers' outing in the late 1920s, destination unknown.

The Dartington Hall stand at the Totnes Show, June 1929. On display were cider, eggs, pottery, basketry, and examples of the wood turner's and the blacksmith's craft.

CHAPTER 13

Events and Celebrations

The Golden Jubilee Celebrations, 1 June 2002

Celebrations started with a fancy dress competition held at Hunter's Moon, the judges being Sybil Newman and Jean and Bill Blinston.

The winner of the girls' competition was Bethany Waistnidge, with Isabella Crouch second and Joyce Potter third.

The villagers follow the procession down Cott Road.

Bill Blinston and Sybil Newman.

Judges Bill and Jean Blinston and Sybil Newman with the winners of the fancy dress competition.

The 'Windsor Oak', planted by Revd Neil Batcock.

Joan Sutcliffe, a village resident all her life.

The boys' competition was won by Jamie and Alex Williams, with Douglas Stokes coming second and Patrick Bourke third.

The procession was led by Larry Hayek in a vintage car, carrying jubilee king and queen Jordan Winters and Amy Finn, with attendants Daniel Smaldon and Chelsea Boon. They were followed by the Sambaluca Band, while villagers and families brought up the rear. The procession followed a route down Cott Road and Forder Lane, past Forder House and into the Dorothy Elmhirst playing-field.

The Revd Neil Batcock and his wife, Katherine, opened the celebrations. Following his planting of a commemorative oak tree, there were sports and

Celebrations outside the church.

Golden jubilee medal and crown.

Colin Osborne with daughter, Lisa, Silver Jubilee 1977.

The egg and spoon race, Golden Jubilee 2002.

Crowds gather to witness Princess Anne's arrival at the Robins Respite Centre.

Robins Respite Centre.

entertainments, and the many stalls, including the ice cream concession, were kept busy on this warm summer's day.

In the evening there was a good attendance at the Meadowbrook Centre for the disco and prize draw.

A Royal Visitor

On 4 February 2000 Princess Anne officially opened Robins, the Respite and Life-Skills Centre in the village. The ten-bedroomed centre had been completed in July 1999.

On her arrival at the £600,000 complex, the Princess Royal was greeted by the Lord Lieutenant of Devon, the High Sheriff, MP for Totnes, Anthony Steen, and the Centre Manager, Richard Hanlon, as well as by cheering pupils from the nearby village schools and their parents. At the entrance the Princess Royal unveiled a plaque commemorating the event and toured the building, meeting care staff.

Events and Celebrations

A Christmas party at the Old Parsonage, 1929.

A New Year's Eve party in the Great Hall, 1949.

Events and Celebrations

A day's outing in the late 1940's. Left to right, back row: *Beryl Gill, Joan Western, Hilda Gill, Peggy Western, Peggy Skedgell, Vera Anstiss;* front: *Ruby and Owen Western with their sons, Stuart and Owen.*

Approaching Shinner's Bridge is Carnival Queen Betty Sercombe, with attendants Jean Hill (left) *and Mary Clark, c.1949.*

Events and Celebrations

The Woodlands Department annual gathering, 1958. The photo includes Mrs Cornish; Mr and Mrs F. Dawe; Mr and Mrs L. R. Elmhirst; Mr and Mrs J. Fulcher; Mr W, Hiley OBE; Mrs Hoare; Mr and Mrs J. James; Mr H. Mills; Mr R. Penn; Mrs Pownsland; Mr and Mrs S. Bunce; Mr P. Sutcliffe; Mr Turner; Mr and Mrs T. Webber.

A Christmas/New Year party in the 1950s. The photograph includes Ken Prowse, Betty Sercombe, Lola and Hetti Denham, Barbara Everett, Roy Bolt, Douglas Harding, Bram and John Bartlett, Ellen Tuffnell, Josie Popplestone, Desmond Rogers, John Fulcher and Beryl Gill.

Events and Celebrations

Coronation celebrations, 2 June 1953. From left to right: *Mrs Noden, ?, Mrs Clake, Ida Barnes, Jock Clark, Mrs Boscence, Jennifer Barnes, Ann Noden.* (Totnes Image Bank and Rural Archive)

Woodlands Department workers and their wives on a day trip down the River Dart in the 1960s. The photograph includes *Mr and Mrs J. James, Mrs Cornish, Mr and Mrs C. Cordy, Mr and Mrs T. Webber, Mr and Mrs P. Foal, Mr and Mrs S. Bunce and Mrs Fulcher.*

Events and Celebrations

Jeanette Denham at the door of the Cott Inn during the silver jubilee parade, 1977.

Left: *Dartington silver jubilee mug.*

Bill and Jean Blinston passing the Cott Inn on 7 June 1977, during the parade to celebrate Her Majesty Queen Elizabeth's silver jubilee.

Redlake trumpeters celebrate the Silver Jubilee. From left: David Denham, David Bitner, Mark Hooker, Richard Denham, Kaeran Hooker.

Events and Celebrations

Celebrating St Mary's Church centenery, 1880–1980. are, from left: Rachel Reed, Mrs Robinson, William 'Bill' Blinston, Lesley Fosbrook, Mrs Turner.

Right: *William 'Bill' Blinston and Sybil Newman at the centenary celerations.*

Redlake street party, to welcome home Tony Covachich (RN) from the Falklands War in 1982. The photograph includes: Mr and Mrs Mason with Philip, Jonathon and Amanda; William, Tessa, Kirsty and Louise MacLening; Mervyn, Carol and Timothy Michelmore; Mrs MacTaggart and Tim; Mary and Jeremy Wood; Julia, Steven and Caroline Roberts; Colin, Betty and Lisa Osborne; Jeanette, Richard, David and Peter Denham; Tony Covachich and family; John Bassett; Brenda and Sarah Lilley; Charlie, Jackie and Theresa Dawe; Mrs and Mrs Jones, Marie and Scott; Jan, Mia and Tammy Frost; Rick Jackie, Claire, David and Josie Bitner.

Events and Celebrations

Left: *Tony Beard (BBC Radio Devon's 'The Wag from Widdecombe') visiting Forder House in the 1990s.*

Right: *The Dartington mug produced in 1995 to celebrate 50 years of peace.*

CHAPTER 14

HMS *Dartington*

HMS *Dartington*, a Ton class coastal minesweeper with a complement of 27, was launched on 22 December 1953.

During the early 1960s she was attached to the 6th Minesweeping Squadron, Singapore. She was also engaged in piracy patrolling around Borneo, Brunei and Sarawak and was the last Royal Navy warship to leave Borneo after the Indonesian Confrontation.

In 1958 the officers and crew of HMS *Dartington* paid a courtesy visit to the village.

She was sold out of service in 1970.

HMS Dartington *emblem.*

HMS Dartington *plaque.*

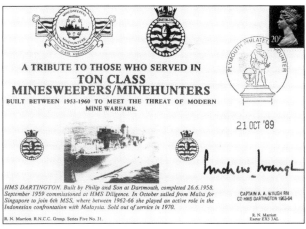

Cover signed by Capt. A.A. Waugh, Commanding Officer HMS Dartington *1963–64.*

HMS Dartington *in the 1960s.*

HMS Dartington *Christmas card, 1960.*

Beacon bungalow, 1935. My first rides were on the motorcycle's petrol tank.

Me on my mother's lap (left), with Maurice (13), my Swiss uncle, and my Swiss grandmother with Claire, a cousin, on her lap, 1937.

CHAPTER 15

My Memories of Dartington
by the Author

When my parents first married they lived at Beacon Bungalow, Yarner, where my father worked at the nearby poultry farm. My mother looked after the first children to attend Foxhole School until I was born, two years later. Father played for Dartington United for several years. In February 1938 we moved to Glen View, a wooden bungalow on the Plymouth Road, near Rattery, where we paid 7s.6d. a week rent and where a well in the back garden, with a bucket on a rope, supplied our water. The bungalow was demolished in 2003 and Oakwood House now stands on its site. With the war in Europe becoming a reality, father would evidently be called up, so in August 1939 we came back to the village, residing temporarily at 'Great Gardens', Old Parsonage, where I remember being fitted with my gas-mask – much to my disgust.

In January 1940 I started school at Shinner's Bridge Primary, taking my essential gas-mask every day. We had to wear them for five minutes each day, not a very comfortable experience, as the visor would get misted up, and I used to discreetly slide my index finger under the edge to let in a bit of fresh air.

When the Duke of Kent visited the sawmills as a guest of the Elmhirsts in 1940, pupils were allowed to line the boundary wall to cheer and wave as his car passed by. In 1941 there were five MacLenings at the school (maybe a record?).

When school dinners eventually started, food came in large round containers, delivered by van,

and Mrs Denham and Mrs Poplestone were two of the ladies who helped serve the meals in the school hut. In one amusing incident (although Miss Murch didn't think it was), during a morning break-time, I was chasing Tony Newson in the playground when, rounding a corner, I collided with Jean King, who was carrying a pile of dinner plates to the hut. Jean survived, but a number of the plates didn't, and cost me a few break-times being kept in!

During the early 1940s, milk from Parnell Newman's Smithfield Farm was delivered in churns by Fran Miller, a jolly fellow, in his pony and trap, and ladled out into householders' jugs. When the farm closed, the round was taken over by Veale Bros. of Whiteley Farm, who delivered with a car towing a trailer. The milk was then in half-pint and pint bottles with cardboard tops. During the severe winter of 1946/47, until the roads were cleared, it was delivered by horse-drawn sledge.

During the war years, those who didn't have an

My early interest in football, 1936.

With my parents at Beacon bungalow, Yarner, in 1936.

The MacLening family picnicking beside the River Dart, Summer 1941. Extreme left: *Mike, Belinda Eary* (back to camera), *Linda her mother, Gerald* (with hat). *Standing* ? (evacuee boy), *Audrey, Cecile with Edward.* Sitting: *William* (cross-legged), *Claire (author's mother), Nigel.*

Paddling in the River Dart, Summer 1943. The children are, from left: *Gerald, Audrey, Nigel, Edward, Cecile, Mike, William;* front: *Belinda.*

Sawpit Lane, May 1985.

A pair of swans on the River Dart, 1942.

underground shelter in their garden (and I don't believe many did), sheltered under either the stairs or a table when the siren sounded on the nights German aircraft were in the area. My refuge in Cott Cross Cottage was under the stairs, where my mother kept our emergency food store. Here I would sit on a stool, a blanket wrapped around me, shivering, with a candle for light (and warmth!), waiting for the 'all-clear' to sound so I could return to my warm bed. Sometimes enemy aircraft were heard droning high overhead on their way to raid Bristol, Cardiff or Swansea.

Often, on Sunday mornings in the summers of 1941–43, weather permitting, the Macs families would load rucksacks with sandwiches, home-made buns, water and a kettle, then walk to the River Dart and spend the day picnicking, paddling, catching tiddlers and thoroughly enjoying ourselves, returning home in the evening tired out.

The arrival of the American troops in 1943 meant exciting times for the village kids, the GI's freely parting with chewing-gum and candy, or a tin of fruit for 'mom', a pack of cigarettes for 'yer dad'. More and more arrived in early '44, and we watched from the playground as US Engineers constructed a water-tank testing pool next to the school. I remember one day, after it was completed, seeing Allied Commanders Eisenhower, Bradley and Montgomery, watching Sherman tanks going through the pool. At break-times we would lean over the wall and chat to the tank crews waiting their turn to be tested. The phrase 'Got any gum, chum?' became quite common, and many a pupil was chastised for chewing in class! The friendly generosity of the GIs was emphasised one Saturday morning, when word got around of an American convoy parked in Sawpit Lane. Several of us arrived as they were cooking breakfast on the field-kitchen burners. Mess tins, knives and forks were thrust into our hands as we joined them in the 'chow' line; sitting alongside them, we tucked into eggs, frankfurters, sweetcorn, baked beans and fresh baked bread, finishing off with a couple of their tasty doughnuts. In May, tented camps were set up in fields in and around the village, as units of the US 4th Infantry Division moved in. With my cousins, Nigel and William, I spent many an hour on Camp XI, at the junction of Wrenford Lane and Plymouth Road, Yarner, chatting or listening to GIs as, accompanied by an accordion, banjo or mouth-organ, they had a sing-song – 'Roll me over' was one of their favourites. Little did we realise that in a month's time they would be fighting for their lives on a Normandy beach. Another memory I have is of GIs who were not supposed to be out of camp giving

The author at Newton Abbot, 1950.

On the footplate.

Nigel and me 2s. each to check if there were any 'snowdrops' (US Military Police) around the Cott Inn. On 26 May 1944 visits to our 'chums' came to an abrupt end, as camps were put out of bounds, troops confined and all contact with civilians ceased. Barbed wire was placed across Wrenford Lane at Redlake Cross and, when told by two US military policemen that we couldn't go up there, we returned home sad, but with a packet of chewing-gum each. A week later the 4th Infantry Division had gone. The barbed wire then thrown up into the hedge remained for many years after the war! When a GI gave me a US one cent coin, which he wore with his 'dog tags' around his neck, it started my hobby of collecting coins! When the Americans left, they disposed of a large variety of equipment in the refuse tip, a disused quarry near the Parsonage. We 'rescued' many items, including steel helmets, water bottles, ammunition pouches, gaiters, haversacks and denims. Our mothers washed and shortened the denim trousers, and for many years youngsters around the Cott–Redlake area, re-enacted the Battle of Arnhem at Redlake Cross Bridge and in the surrounding fields: albeit mostly in American dress and with American equipment! Many a boy and girl has run beneath that narrow bridge under 'enemy fire', keeping their head down.

In those bygone years, parents didn't worry about where their children were, knowing they were safe playing. 'They'll come home when they're hungry,' was the saying. Our leisure pursuits included climbing trees, building camps in the woods, playing in the stream, playing cowboys and Indians, roller-skating and, occasionally, being chased out of farmer Codd's fields, either by him or by labourer Percy Barnes. We never did stop to ask the reason why – it was not as if we left gates open, and always climbed over them. 'Scrumping' apples was probably the naughtiest thing we did. It was best to avoid the village 'bobby,' if possible, even if you were behaving yourself. Peering at you with the questioning look that policemen had in those days, he would usually ask, 'And what are you up to?'. Now and again, usually on Saturday afternoons, we visited Totnes cinema, which burned down in March 1944. Front seats were 9d., centre seats 1s., back rows 1s.9d. and upstairs 2s.6d. We would purchase a 9d. ticket then, when the lights were dimmed and the film started, go to the toilet and return to sit in the 1s. seats. If you were spotted by an usherette, she usually made you go back to your proper seat, but if there were plenty of empty seats and a 'good' usherette on duty, she would turn a blind eye and let you stay, 'As long as you are quiet!'.

Perhaps not the happiest of characters was the elderly Mrs Champernowne, who lived at Vineyard. She rode her horse sidesaddle around the area of Staple and Cott, and was prone to ordering children

154

and adults alike to, 'Get out of the way!'. Her ancestors having once ruled the parish for 400 years, maybe she liked to think they still did! When the American troops established a gun site in her field, the story went that the lady, approaching them armed with her shotgun, ordered them out. Turning their gun on her, the Americans replied, 'Mam if we fire this, you will disappear!' She quickly left.

I had my allocation of chores to do. I had to feed the chickens and the two pet rabbits in the mornings before going to school and again when I returned in the afternoon, and collect the eggs. In the winter months it was my job to light the fire, and I cleaned out the rabbit hutch on Saturday mornings and, every other Saturday, the chicken house, digging over their run. I also had to blacken the stove, clean the flue and chop enough kindling sticks for the week. With the wireless run on a large 'dry' battery and accumulator, my job on Thursdays, after school, was to take the accumulator to the garage next to the Central Office, to be recharged (this cost 6d.) and collect the charged-up one. With my parents working and me at school, our door was left unlocked all day. The baker would leave bread on the table, while the Co-op grocery list would be left for Mr Heath to sit down and write the order. The baker delivered on Thursdays, leaving the box of groceries on the table and picking up the money. The insurance money was also left out – never a problem in those days. It was often said, until war broke out, that some householders never even locked their doors at night!

In 1945, with the war ended, I joined the Scouts and left Primary School to continue my education at Totnes Secondary School. League football commenced the following year, and during the soccer season, on Saturday afternoons, father and I would watch Torquay United or, if they were playing away, would travel to either Plymouth Argyle or Exeter City. Collecting football programmes became a hobby with many schoolboys, me included. I still have some, but at one time had at least one from every league club in England and Wales, most of those from Scotland and many Irish programmes.

For my eleventh birthday I received a bicycle,

which cost £11.2s.0d., plus 2s9d. for the bell. I put the bike to good use, especially after leaving school, often cycling the 11½ miles to Newton Abbot locomotive depot at all times of the night and day and in all kinds of weather – a lonely road in those days! As we reached our teens, soccer became a ritual. On Sunday mornings there was a regular gathering at the playing-fields for a kick-about, with an occasional match against Totnes Youth Club or Foxhole School on a Sunday afternoon. Lads I remember playing alongside me are Bram and John Bartlett, Derek Bennett, Derek Clark, Tony Guy, Keith Hocking, Nigel MacLening, Ashley and Edgar Miller, Alan Parnell, Terry Parsons, Brian Piller, David Rafferty, Ken Selleck, Bernard Taylor, Len Webber and Fred Widger.

In January 1953, when HM Government required my services for two years, I endured the first three months of 'square bashing' (and no leave) and quickly learned to keep my eyes and ears open and my mouth shut! During my service, being tall, I was always one of a dozen lads selected as guard of honour to visiting brigadiers or generals, including, on one occasion, Maj.-Gen. Jacques de Dixunde, of the Belgian Army.

Travelling home on leave was often a bit of a problem if arriving at Newton Abbot late at night, there being no train to Totnes until morning. On three occasions I decided to walk the 11½ miles. The first time a taxi driver picked me up at Two Mile Oak and dropped me at Totnes Plains, with no charge! The second time I walked the whole way, arriving home just after 1a.m., tapping on my parents' bedroom window with the clothes prop to wake them! On the third occasion, after a day knee-deep in snow on a map-reading exercise on Salisbury Plain, I was granted a 48-hour pass and arrived in Newton Abbot after 1a.m. and, 'footing it' to Dartington, arrived home at 2.45a.m., again using the prop to tap on my parents' bedroom window!

Although my residence in the village came to an end in 1956, after 22 years, I frequently visited my parents for the next 30 years and the cottage still has many memories for me. Today, after 75 years, there are still MacLenings living in the village.

The six MacLening brothers with their mother, 1930 From left: *George (Jeff), Stuart, Owen, Nelson, Enos and Robert (Bob).*

Pierre and Marie Pont with their five daughters in Switzerland in the early 1920s. Left to right, back row: *Jeanne, Cecile,* middle: *Germaine, Clara;* front: *Annette.*

CHAPTER 16

My Family History
by the Author

MACLENING

Sept of MacLennan
Origin of name: Gaelic son of Finnan's servant

Motto: Dum Spiro Spero (While I breathe, I hope)

The family plaque.

My family name has been spelled or altered in many different ways over the centuries. Tradition relates that the family is descended from the Logans of Drumderfit, in Easter Ross, in the Highlands of Scotland.

In the fifteenth century a feud between the Logans and the Frasers ended in a bloody battle at North Kessock, in which Gilligorm, the chief of the Logans, was killed and his widow carried off by the victors. She gave birth to a posthumous son of Gilligorm, a son who, from his deformity, was known as Crotair MacGilligorm. He was educated by the Monks at Beauly Priory, in Scotland and, on reaching manhood, took Holy Orders at Kilmor in Sleat and in Kilchrinin, Glenelg. Like many others of the Highland clergy at that period, he did not remain celibate and his descendants came to be known as Siol Fhinnein, or MacLennans. During the Battle of

Auldearn in 1645 they acted as standard bearers to Lord Seaforth, and many were killed in their gallant defence of the standard.

In Scotland the spelling of surnames only really began to be consistent after compulsory registration in 1855. Before that date, the session clerk, as a rule, wrote down what he heard, or thought he heard, many families being unable to read or write, and would spell the names as he chose. The intermingling of a variety of regional dialects, together with the Gaelic spoken by the Highlanders and Islanders, made his job even more difficult.

A John MacLenane mentioned in 1529, and an Adam MacLenane in 1586, are possibly my ancestors.

My great-great-great-great-grandfather, James MacLennan/McLellan, only lived a short life, from 1725 to 1750.

Alexander McLellan/McLenan, my great-great-great grandfather, married Mary Kennedy in August 1768 in Cluny, Invernesshire. They had six children, the first two spelling their surname McLinen, the next McLennan and the last three McLellan.

My great-great-grandfather, Donald McLellan, born in 1777, enlisted in the Army in Edinburgh at the age of 16, and in 1805 was serving in the Horse Brigade of the Royal Artillery at Woolwich, where he married.

My great-grandfather, George Nelson McLeland was born in Woolwich, and married Mary Chapman (who could neither read nor write) in 1833 in Shoreham, Kent. They had eight children. At some time during his life, under the belief that the family name was misspelt, he restyled it to MacLening. He died in 1893.

My grandfather, William, born in 1850, enlisted for 12 years, at the age of 21, in the Royal Horse Artillery, serving in Alderney (1872–73), India (1876–83) and Afghanistan (Dec 1878–Nov 1880). He married Fanny Young (my grandmother, 16 years his junior) in 1887 at Chiddingstone, Kent. They had 11 children – no TV or central heating in those days! My grandfather died in 1914 and my grandmother in 1957, aged 90.

All six of their boys served in the Armed Forces. Nelson joined the Royal Horse Artillery on his nineteenth birthday, serving in France, Belgium, Palestine and Syria (1914–19). Enos, who, like many others at that time, lied about his age to enlist, also served in France. Captured, he spent two years as a prisoner of war in Germany. Robert enlisted for six years as a farrier in the Horse Artillery, serving in Palestine and

Claire on the steps of the Great Hall after receiving her long service award, June 1973.

Claire's long service award.

Egypt (1921–26). Owen, called-up in 1940, served with the RASC in N. Ireland, France, Belgium, Holland and Germany (1944–45). He was with the first troops to enter Belsen concentration camp in April 1945. George was invalided out of the Royal Artillery in 1941. Stuart served on the battleship HMS *Anson*, escorting Arctic convoys to Russia (1942–44) and then in the Far East (1945–46).

My father, George, or 'Jeff', as he was mostly known, worked at various jobs after coming to Dartington, including as a poultryman. He was also involved in the building of Totnes Senior School and of Totnes bypass, then, after being invalided out of the Army, was employed at Totnes shipyard, where wooden acoustic minesweepers were built. Followed this, he helped build landing-craft for D-Day on the old racecourse site and, after the war, worked on the completion of the bypass bridge over the railway, on which project a group of German prisoners of war were also employed. He also worked at Gravley (USA) Overseas at Buckfastleigh and at John Crook motorcycle repair shop, and was groundsman at Foxhole School. He died in 1988, a month before his 78th birthday, after suffering with Parkinson's disease for many years.

My mother, Clara-Marie (née Pont), was born in a wooden chalet on the outskirts of Gryon, a small mountain village in French-speaking Switzerland, the second eldest of five girls and a brother. Clara (Claire) first came to England on holiday, then, in the latter years of the 1920s, four of the sisters and a cousin came to take up employment in this country. They all eventually married Englishmen, two of the sisters marrying two brothers. Claire came to Dartington in 1931, followed by George 'Jeff' MacLening shortly after. They married in August the following year and for over 40 years she worked at various times for Dartington Hall Trustees, at Foxhole and Aller Park schools, at the Dance School and the Arts Department, at the Social Centre works canteen and at the sawmills during the early years of the war. Retiring in June 1973, aged 65, she died in 1999, aged 91.

Subscribers

Irene and Eric Adams, Dartington, Devon

Lorna Arscott, Aberdeen, Scotland

Adrian Arscott, Totnes, Devon

Joyce, John, Nick and Amanda Bailey, Dartington

Patrick John Baker-Blight, Broad View, Dartington

Gwen Barrett, Dibden Purlieu, Hants

Mary and Lucy Bartlett, Dartington Hall, Devon

Emma Bartlett, Hamilton, New Zealand

Anthony and Wendy Beard

Ian and Susan Bishop, Dartington

Jeremy Michael Blight, Broad View, Dartington

Anita Winter & Jeremy Blight, Dartington

Peter Booth, Ashburton

Stephen Bristow and Kay Dunbar, Droridge Farm, Dartington

Stan and Iris Brock

K. J. Burrow, Bucks Cross, Devon

Mrs Betty E. Clark (née Sercombe), Paignton, Devon

Mr Stanley R. Clements, Dartington, Devon

Mr Ray & Mrs Liz Clements, Dartington

Geraldine Coker, Ipplepen, Devon

Caroline Cole, Paignton, Devon

Kevin Cordy, Upper Caldecote, Bedfordshire

David Cordy, Baldock, Hertfordshire

Joyce Patricia Coulson, Barnsley, South Yorkshire

Jack Crago, Week, Dartington

Antonia Del Mar, Dartington, Devon

Morwenna Del Mar, Dartington, Devon

Gary Dingle, Eastington, Glos

Penny Dow, Dartington, Devon

Laurence J. Edwards, Dartington, Devon

Brian C. Evans, Dartington, Devon

Andrew and Kim Frankland, Vineyard

Samantha French, Torquay, Devon

Gallon Family, Dartington, Devon

Stuart Giles, Dartington, Devon

John and Chris Gordon, Belleigh, Dartington

Edwin W.E. Guy, Dartington, Devon

David A. Guy, Marldon, Devon

Margaret A. Hatch, Dartington, Devon

June Hext (née Walters)

Peter and Margaret Hodge, Ivybridge, Devon

Mrs Jan L. Holland (née Winter), Dartington, Devon

Ada. R. J. Horswill

Jeanette A. Howard (née Widger), Dartington

David James, Thurlbear, Taunton

Kevin James, Taunton

Pat Jerred (née Cole), Dartington

Steve and Tricia Jones, Redlake, Dartington

Val M. Keel (née Lake)

Mr Tony & Mrs Rene Kerswell (née Clements), Buckfastleigh

Chantal Kickx, Dartington

Alice M. M. Knowles, Dartington, Devon

Graham Knowles

John and Marlene Laskey, Chudleigh

June Margaret Louise Lindridge, Andover, Hampshire

Stephen MacLening, Camberley, Surrey

Rebecca MacLening, Camberley, Surrey

Christopher MacLening, Camberley, Surrey

Elizabeth Marriott, Broughton Astley, Leics

Philip and Valerie Munro, Hop Cottage, Staple,
Dartington

Tracey (Majeske) Neville, Hawaii, USA

Audrey C. Neville, Mandurah, Western
Australia

Alistair J. Neville, Parkwood, Western Australia

Anthony S. Newson, Totnes

Alastair and Jill Paramore, Clay Lane,
Dartington

Pamela K.C. Parnell, Plymouth, Devon

Sandra Payne (Dingle), Dartington, Devon

Mrs Rosemary A. Piller, Torquay, Devon

Maurice Pont, Gryon, Switzerland

Michael K. Pound, Dartington, Devon

Julia M. Roberts, Dartington, Devon

Sylvia. M.M. Rogers, Dartington

K. Rosser, Dartington

Selina Sharp (née Crook), Charlie & Mafalda
Winson, Dartington, Devon

Clare Showell (née Bunce)

Ray and Jennifer Simmonds, Malta

Viola Standen, Paignton, Devon

Mavis Starbuck (née Winson) and Pat Crook
(née Winson), Sisters from Dartington, Devon

Mrs Judith Talbot, Ivybridge, Devon

D. and L. Teague, Spain

Graham Thorne, Maldon

Sharon Vincent, Dartington

Mr Ed & Mrs Lyn Wall (née Clements), South
Brent

John F.W. Walling, Newton Abbot, Devon

Judy Webber

Iris M. H. Webber (née Tucker), Dartington

Josephine Welch (née Kellock), Allerton,
Dartington, Devon

Fred Widger, Totnes, Devon

Chris, Lisa, Jamie and Alex Williams,
Dartington

Mr W. George and Mrs Shirley Winter (née
Clements), Dartington, Devon